T0285709

"I've laughed. I've cried. It's the best book Joe Bonsall has EVER written. Not only will the reader see Joe—they will see THEMSELVES in a profound manner through his masterful writing. LOVE IT!!
—**Scott McKain**, Hall of Fame speaker
and author of *The Ultimate Customer Experience*

"When I was a teenager, I had a really high singing voice and thought it wasn't good. One day, I heard Joe Bonsall hitting the high notes on 'Elvira' and saw how everyone loved his sound. It gave me the confidence to move forward with my own singing! I've become friends with Joe over the years, and I've never met a more humble and genuine person than him. Country fans are going to LOVE this book! It's a must read!"

—**John Rich**

"Joe is one of my heroes in the industry. I see myself in his story—from struggles to overcoming adversity—it's truly inspiring. Read this memoir if you want to be encouraged and hear Joe's own amazing rescue story—you don't want to miss this book."

—**Zach Williams**

"For someone who 'can't build a campfire,' this city boy from 3517 Jasper Street has brought a lot of joy and happiness to millions of people—and I mean millions . . . And a few cats, too. His spiritual strength and love for his Country, Family, and Friends is a great example for all of us to live by. I'm proud to call Joe my friend."

—**Joe West**

"It's always been my contention that you only get to know someone when you are privy to hearing them tell their life story in small bits and pieces. Without these special moments you only know a part of the story, but with them the patchwork quilt that is their life becomes complete.

"Few people are as instantly recognizable as the Oak Ridge Boys' tenor Joe Bonsall. In the world of entertainment, he is a legend. But he is so much more than that. Joe is open, honest, positive, upbeat, and completely transparent. He is a person constantly searching for purpose and joy. He has always believed in the impossible and has lived to see the impossible become reality time and time again. Along the way he's been quick to thank everyone who's opened the doors that made his dreams come true.

"The series of essays found in between these covers presents the story of a man who never forgot his roots, lived through tragedies, hit wall after wall, and saw each failure as a lesson rather than a stop sign. When his last hurrah was stolen by an illness that is both relentless and unforgiving, he didn't quit living, but rather found new ways to enjoy life and inspire others.

"In these pages, Joe's life is explored in small bits and pieces, and we meet the often unique people and go to the fascinating places that created a person whose joy and music have left a remarkable legacy. Yet, as insightful and entertaining as Joe's story is, I believe *I See Myself*'s greatest gift will be inspiring readers to reflect upon their own lives and remember those who paved the way for the joy and success they have known.

"It's so like Joe to remind us to count our blessings, and he does that time and time again in *I See Myself*."

—**Ace Collins**, bestselling author

"I met Joe Bonsall by chance in the early 90's. The Isaacs were in Nashville recording, and we had the evening off. When I was on my way out of a local mall and saw Joe walking in, I was compelled to stop him and tell him what a big fan of The Oak Ridge Boys music I was. He was so nice and took his time with me. That made a lasting impression on me.

"Fast forward several years and I was asked to produce some records on the Oaks. That's when I really fell in love with all of them. Joe and I especially hit it off because of his love for acoustic and Bluegrass music. We took time on some of the first albums I produced for Joe to record the banjo parts on some of the songs. I enjoyed watching him listen to the finished product. What an amazing time for me! Sometimes you meet people you look up to and wish you had never met them. There are other times you meet people and see they're better than you thought they could be. Joe is that man. Amazing.

"Reading *I See Myself*, I found myself crying, smiling, and laughing as I read all these little short stories from Joe's life. This book has so many great moments that show you why Joe is the man he is today. I loved going down memory lane in each story. I love you, Joe."

—**Ben Isaacs**

"I really enjoyed *I See Myself*. Partly because I've been friends with Joe, Duane, Richard, and William Lee for over 45 years. It is a good, honest insight into Joe's life and easy reading."

—**Jerry Martin**

"Joe Bonsall was a part of 'America's Band,' The Oak Ridge Boys, for over fifty years until his retirement, but his imprint on the music industry will live forever. One of the nicest people in show business, Joe's story is a great American story of a Philadelphia kid from the inner city whose vocal talent took him from rough housing in a tough Philly neighborhood to singing at the White House and in packed venues across the globe. He and his long-standing musical 'brothers,' who formed this legacy act, entertained four generations of fans because their music and their performances never got old or lost their magic. Joe Bonsall's contagious smile and effusive personality helped keep the Oaks relevant through numerous decades of a changing music scene. Two things have never changed—the popularity of The Oak Ridge Boys, and the humility and authenticity of Joe Bonsall. I have loved these guys and have counted it a significant honor to get to know them and see them both on stage and backstage. They are the same guys. Joe's story is one that will bless and encourage you! You already love the music!"

—**Mike Huckabee**

"Harlan Howard famously described country music as '. . . three chords and the truth.' In *I See Myself*, Joe Bonsall offers three words and the truth. This candid and poignant memoir takes readers through a well-lived life. Escorting us onstage, backstage, on tour buses, through the streets of Philly, to exotic locales, hospitals, and cemeteries—Joe offers insights into life, love, patriotism, heartbreak, perseverance, and faith from his extraordinary perspective."

—**Peter Rosenberger**, author/syndicated radio host of *Hope for the Caregiver*, and Joe Bonsall fan

"Joe Bonsall says he sees himself in 'a state of perpetual amazement' when he looks back over the life he's been privileged to live. As his friend I stand in amazement at his embrace-life attitude about everything, which has splashed over on to me and all who know him.

—**Bill Gaither**

"This book is a page turner that will keep you laughing and saying 'wow' over and over and over again."

—**Jimmy Wayne**, recording artist and bestselling author

"This is the book America has been waiting for Joe Bonsall to write! *I See Myself*—the latest offering from this prolific author—is a quiet masterpiece. A repository of reflections and perspective, this is a book with the power to calm and inspire. *I See Myself* is the perfect landing place for people who ponder life and its meaning, and it has been written by a man whose thoughts lead us to a higher plane."

—**Andy Andrews**, New York Times bestselling author of *The Traveler's Gift* and *The Noticer*

"In his book *I See Myself*, Joe Bonsall wrote 'Each life is special, and each life is different one from the other as it relates to roads traveled.' Joe's life was marvelously special. This book is equally so because Joe gave us the gift of sharing his life's highs and lows at a time when he was quite aware that for him the gift of life he'd found exhilarating was coming to an end.

"Backstage at the Grand Ole Opry and via text messages from him sent from coast to coast, Joe reminded me often to love life, to love others, to take nothing for granted, and to laugh mightily. When I saw Joe for the last time at his house overlooking Old Hickory Lake one sunny day not long ago, he looked at me and said he was in absolute awe of the life he'd been fortunate to live and how amazing it had been right up until he started suffering symptoms of the disease that took him from us. I'm in awe of that life, too, and of the fact that Joe has shared it with us in his own words.

"What a gift. What a legacy."

—**Dan Rogers**, executive producer, Grand Ole Opry / grateful friend of Joe Bonsall

I SEE MYSELF

I SEE MYSELF

Musings and Memories of a Blessed Life

Joseph S. Bonsall

FIDELIS
PUBLISHING

FIDELIS PUBLISHING®

ISBN: 9781956454833
ISBN (eBook): 9781956454840

I SEE MYSELF
Musings and Memories of a Blessed Life
© 2024 Joseph S. Bonsall

Cover Design by Diana Lawrence
Interior Layout/Typesetting by Lisa Parnell
Edited by Amanda Varian

Order at www.faithfultext.com for a significant discount. Email info@fidelispublishing.com to inquire about bulk purchase discounts.

Fidelis Publishing, LLC • Winchester, VA / Nashville, TN
fidelispublishing.com

Manufactured in the United States of America

10 9 8 7 6 5 4 3 2 1

FIDELIS
PUBLISHING

DEDICATED TO
those who have stood at the crossroads.

Turn your eyes upon Jesus
Look full in His wonderful face
And the things of earth will grow strangely dim
In the light of His glory and grace.

—Helen H. Lemmel

~

You do not know what may come tomorrow.
For what is your life? It is a vapor, that appears
for a little time, and then vanishes away.

—James 4:14 (author's paraphrase)

~

She gave this name to the Lord who spoke to her:
"You are the God who sees me," for she said,
"I have now seen the One who sees me."

—Genesis 16:13 NIV

Foreword

When I look at Joe Bonsall, I see a life fulfilled. The son of two military veterans, raised to become street-smart in the hood-influenced neighborhood of Philadelphia, Pennsylvania, his parents taught him he could be anything he wished to be if he worked hard, told the truth, and trusted in God.

Joe wanted to sing, so he set his goal to singing, and he sang professionally for over six decades. Joe wanted to write, so he became the author of ten books, including the Molly the Cat series of children's books, *G.I. Joe and Lillie*, and others. Joe wanted to write songs, so he sat down and wrote a catalog of songs. Joe can do anything he sets his mind to do.

But what impresses me the most is the energy, love, and compassion he puts into everything he does and his unique gift to communicate those emotions and feelings into every performance, song, and book.

When I look at Joe Bonsall, I see all the good things I would love to see in myself. Joe is "that" best friend that every person hopes to have in their life.

I love you, Joe,
Duane Allen
Oak Ridge Boys

By Way of Introduction

I am Joe Bonsall. I have been one of the Oak Ridge Boys for over fifty years, and I have authored ten published books before this one.

My life has been very blessed. I grew up on the rough streets of Philadelphia, Pennsylvania, and early interest in four-part southern gospel harmony groups set a course and a dream that eventually led to my being a part of over 41 million albums sold, the Gospel Music Hall of Fame, the Vocal Group Hall of Fame, the Philadelphia Music Alliance Hall of Fame, and most recently the Country Music Hall of Fame, as well as membership in the greatest musical family on earth—the Grand Ole Opry! With my three brothers and singing partners Duane Allen, William Lee Golden, and Richard Sterban, the Oak Ridge Boys have made music history.

Our accomplishments together will, hopefully, live on long after we are gone from this planet, and for this I am so very grateful and thankful. If you have read any of my previous works, you know I always give my Lord and Savior and the King of my life, Jesus Christ, the honor and the glory in all things. All the songs and shows through these years are like so much water running beneath so many bridges.

I see myself existing in a state of perpetual amazement over every single bit of it, and I find myself on my knees quite often just saying, "Thank You, Lord, for these constant blessings that are way beyond any deserving on my part." A music career that continues to thrive even though the "Boys" are no longer boys, an incredible loving, supporting, and beautiful wife, Mary Ann, who is always here for me, two wonderful and beautiful daughters, Jennifer and Sabrina, and two awesome grandkids, Breanne and Luke. Our Breanne has given us a great-grandson, Noah Chance, who is also quite amazing! He may even be president one day.

My mother, Lillie, taught me prayer was important. That you must humble yourself before God and be thankful for all things and to constantly seek His will and guidance in your life. To do that, she would add, you MUST get down on your knees.

As usual, Mommy was right, and in my mind's eye I can still see her whispering prayers on behalf of my sister, Nancy, and me as she knelt by her bedside in the upstairs front bedroom in the little row house where we grew up. It is no wonder that my life has turned out well.

I sing and I enjoy writing. I live in Hendersonville, Tennessee, with my Mary and five wonderful cats. We also own a farm on the TN/KY line and, much to the dismay of our cats, I play the banjo.

I see myself writing more detailed accounts of all this stuff and much more within the pages of this little book you are holding. Thank you for reading.

I began to write this book at the end of 2020, which was a tough time for all of us. That Covid thing changed the world, and the very uncertainty of it all was quite paralyzing, especially for those of little faith. However, in those days and into the present I have been looking inward more than ever.

I have been reflecting on my life, my loves, my experiences, my career, my dreams, and perhaps gazing into the glass a bit and wondering what my life may come to be in whatever future

I have left on this earth. At seventy-three years old (now seventy-six in 2024) I realize there are many more years behind me than what lies ahead. And I am good with this revelation.

Life is God's greatest gift to us this side of salvation and the promise of heaven. And it must be honored and respected as such. Each life and each person are important and, dare I say it, "ALL lives DO matter to God." He loves each one of us, and the price paid upon the cross by His only begotten Son, Jesus, and the salvation and eternal life promised by a risen Savior are there for the asking—no matter what color you may be.

Red and yellow, black, and white, ALL are precious in His sight. That little song from childhood still applies regardless of what your cable news station says.

But enough preaching.

They say before death, or perhaps during death, our lives pass before our eyes, and we can picture a kind of movie screen where these scenes play out in our conscious or subconscious minds. Of course, there has never been any definitive proof of this. I have had several dear friends whose heart just stopped, and they were gone from this earth before their body hit the ground, so I doubt there was time for them to reflect much on days that had passed.

This is not a narrative or even a wonderment concerning my last breath but more of a good, hard look at random visions, which have, of late, manifested themselves from just behind the curtain. Yes, each life is special, and each life is different as it relates to roads traveled. I move forward here with my own sort of autobiographical musings written at different times, and I hope some might find it all worthy enough to read.

Since I wrote *G.I. Joe and Lillie* in the early 2000s, many have urged me to write a sequel or an autobiography explaining how a Philly boy ended up as an Oak Ridge Boy, and I have always put it off. But I think I have now found a fun way to write about myself and the Oak Ridge Boys.

Remember those blue people in the movie *Avatar*? Remember the big, tall blue woman? She would say, "I see you. I see you," and what she meant was "I really see inside of you." Not just, "I see you." But "I SEE you."

I had a dream one night, and I heard her in the dream. Then I heard myself saying, "I see myself . . . I see myself," and that gave me the idea on how to write the book.

There is no rhyme or reason to the timetable here, as you will quickly ascertain. *I See Myself* is just a collection of visions as I have searched through my mental archives and they have manifested themselves, reminding me of a life well lived. I have simply followed the leads and written stuff down. I hope these little musings and memories will entertain and, hopefully, inspire you to follow your dreams.

Turn the pages and ride with me for a little while.

CHAPTER 1

I see myself always being quite joyful and a bit teary-eyed to be planting my feet back upon the solid ground of the United States of America.

I see myself eating fondue and sipping a glass of cabernet in Gruyere, Switzerland, on the balcony of a small hostel in a beautiful valley staring up at the Alps. I have seen many photos and films of the Alps, but seeing them in person was quite invigorating.

The Oak Ridge Boys have not traveled overseas very often, but each time we have it has been memorable. On this Swiss occasion we were there to film a piece for a network television show about country music around the world. We taped a Beatles *Help!* sort of video utilizing the song "Come on In (Baby Take Your Coat Off)," and it was fun.

I wonder where that old film might be today. Four young Oak Ridge Boys running through the Swiss Alps and all over the storybook town of Gruyere, lip-synching and acting like crazy fools for the camera. After being the Beatles for two days, we traveled to Lake Geneva for the famous Montreux Jazz Festival, where the audience loved Roy Clark—and absolutely hated us and Barbara Mandrell.

Barbara cried and ran off the stage. We first got a bit angry and then laughed about it. That was enough of Switzerland, as far as I was concerned.

I see myself in London several times, and on one of those occasions we played the Royal Albert Hall for two consecutive nights with Johnny Mathis. I listened to his whole show each night and was blown away both times by his masterful vocals. We met him once before in Philadelphia for the Bicentennial Celebration of America in 1976. But to sit in the balcony and hear that man sing was unforgettable!

"Chances are . . ."

I see myself singing in Nice, France, where we opened the great Acropolis Performance Center—the Palais des Congrès Acropolis—on American Music Night and donated the proceeds of the show to a wonderful organization called Feed the Children. The money was used to dig four water wells in our names in the Rift Valley of Kenya, Africa. Yes, there is a Joe Bonsall water well in Kenya. Entire towns were built around those wells. Where there is water, there is life.

Next, there was a country television show in Munich, Germany, and a music festival in Brussels, Belgium, where we followed a punk rock band who threw up on the piano, and the following night a terrorist group blew up the stage.

That was close.

We taped a huge network television show in Monaco with the Royal Family in attendance—and there was a once-in-a-lifetime Soviet Union tour with Roy Clark, where we played shows in Riga, Latvia, Moscow, and the city formerly called Leningrad.

We have also toured all over Scandinavia doing shows in Denmark, Sweden, Norway, and Finland. We never made it to Asia or even to Australia or New Zealand.

I see myself always being quite joyful and a bit teary-eyed to plant my feet back upon the solid ground of the United States of America. No matter how attractive world travel may seem to be, I would rather be doing shows in the United States and Canada than taking trips overseas.

One of the few times our management has ever gotten upset with me is when I turned down an offer to play a festival in Bulgaria. My point was we hadn't played in San Diego in over ten years, so I preferred we book San Diego instead of Sofia.

CHAPTER 2

I have never to this day won anything in my entire life except for that bicycle. There are usually no free lunches, just hard work.

I see myself riding my new English Racer, three-speed bike through my Philly neighborhood streets. I won it in a raffle on a Saturday afternoon on Vampire Movie Day at The Midway Theater, and I had to walk it the four blocks to my house because the tires were flat.

I also had to convince my father that I hadn't stolen it. I have never to this day won anything in my entire life except for that bicycle. There are usually no free lunches, just hard work. But on this day, I WON a bike, and I have never forgotten it.

They gave away a bicycle every Saturday during the summer at the Midway Theater. All the stores on Kensington Avenue gave out tickets with a purchase, and that week I had bought a new pair of shoes from Thom McAn and had about twelve tickets in my pocket. Some kids had a shoebox full of tickets. In between movies, a guy in a tuxedo came out with the bike and announced the winning number. What a feeling to hold the winning number! I gave my old Schwinn dinosaur bike to an even poorer kid on Clearance Street.

Christopher Lee, Peter Cushing, Bela Lugosi, and a new bike all in one afternoon. A pretty good day in the neighborhood.

CHAPTER 3

I would go by myself most of the time, sit in the balcony, and chow down on buttered popcorn and Goldenberg's Peanut Chews.

I see myself loving movies. When I was just eleven or twelve, my first job was working at Betty Angelino's luncheonette where I went from stocking shelves and carrying bottles of soda up and down the stairs from the basement to being a waiter and short order cook. I could make a mean cheesesteak.

Now, I loved Betty, but she never did pay very much, so I augmented my little salary by waiting outside of the Acme Supermarket on Kensington Avenue with my little red wagon, and I would help old ladies take their groceries home. I was Instacart before Instacart!

They usually paid twenty-five cents—or perhaps fifty cents if I carried their groceries into the house. I would even help them put the stuff away. I usually built up a nice stash of movie money.

We had two theaters in the neighborhood: The Iris on Kensington Avenue and The Midway on Allegheny Avenue. I would go by myself most of the time, sit in the balcony, and chow down on buttered popcorn and Goldenberg's Peanut Chews.

I saw *The Ten Commandments* and *Ben Hur* about ten times each. I saw every horror movie ever made and every John

Wayne movie released during that time, my favorite being *The Comancheros*.

"Mon Sewer . . . you ARE a Lulu."

Believe it or not, I loved *West Side Story*. I used to dream about being on Broadway. As Tony, I would run through the streets singing "Maria." But that ship sailed long ago.

It's a wonder though I never took up acting and that music took precedence in my life. As a side note, there was a beautiful new theater in the northeast section of Philly called Mayfair, which was way north of us. Once my mother talked my father into driving us all up there to this Mayfair Theater to see *Gone with the Wind*, which was, at that time, the longest movie ever made. I think it lasted twelve hours—at least it felt like it. My father would have rather gone back to Utah Beach on D-Day than sit through that film. But he did, sort of. He went to the men's room for a smoke at least twenty-five times, or so it seemed.

After the movie we all ate at the Mayfair Diner, which to us was like dining at a five-star restaurant. Daddy loved the chicken croquettes there, and years later after his stroke when I came home to visit, I would drive him up to the Mayfair Diner— just me and him—and treat him to some croquettes . . . a nice memory.

CHAPTER 4

I see myself standing just behind the curtain on The Tonight Show *set waiting to be introduced by Johnny Carson.*

I see myself standing just behind the curtain on *The Tonight Show* set waiting to be introduced by Johnny Carson. As a veteran of the stage, I don't usually get very nervous, but *The Tonight Show* was an entirely different ballgame for all the Oak Ridge Boys.

As Johnny sat at his famous desk with Ed McMahon by his side, we could hear him say, "Here they are, ladies and gentlemen, the Grammy–award-winning group we have all come to love singing their new single, 'Leaving Louisiana in the Broad Daylight' . . . THE OAK RIDGE BOYS!"

I felt like I was going to faint. My palms were so sweaty it was downright embarrassing. But it always turned out to be a blessing, because appearing on over thirty *Tonight Shows* over the years and premiering single after single on Johnny Carson helped us go from being an award-winning country group to a household name.

We heard that Johnny didn't like to talk to musical acts, so we always opted to do a second song instead of asking for couch time with him. However, we would always sit and talk and laugh with a guest host.

I remember John Davidson, Roy Clark, and Kenny Rogers filling in for Johnny—that was always fun because we really knew those guys. Carson, although always gracious, was a bit shy and hard to get to know unless you were Don Rickles or Robin Williams.

Over the 1970s and well into the '80s, our manager and godfather, Jim Halsey, had an amazing West Coast operation. A cracker jack television agent named Dick Howard pulled off miracle after miracle getting us on *The Tonight Show* before we ever had a hit record. We also did close to thirty Mike Douglas and Merv Griffin shows, and we appeared on *The Dinah Shore Show* so often we became known as Dinah's Darlings.

If you add up all the big, major network appearances in those days, including *Dukes of Hazzard* and the Minnie Pearl Christmas specials, it seemed like the Oak Ridge Boys were in your living room every week. Dick Howard called it "building the foundation" that would carry the Oaks to the top of the business and provide longevity. Dick Howard was correct. I miss him.

When "Elvira" hit in 1981, we broke the song on *The Tonight Show*, and it went over big-time. The audience stood up, the cameramen and even Doc Severinsen and his entire band were singing it with us! One of the secrets to the success of "Elvira" was that people knew it was the Oak Ridge Boys singing it, and Johnny Carson got that all started for us. 🎤

CHAPTER 5

If I ever go bald, my scarred-up head will make me look like I just escaped from prison.

I see myself getting the cornbread crap kicked out of me by a bunch of bullies while walking home from John Paul Jones Junior High School and arriving home with my head split open and bleeding like a stuck pig. My mother took me to the hospital to get stitches in my head. I see myself never walking by that corner ever again!

I have had many stitches sewn into my head over the years even while on the road with the Oaks. One time while getting into the back of a van in California, I tore the top of my head open and bled everywhere as a head wound is wont to do. An ambulance and a fire engine arrived as our long-time keyboard genius Ronnie Fairchild was suppressing the wound with a table-cloth he had retrieved from the hotel where we were staying. All the blood was freaking everybody out. It looked more like a drive-by shooting than a stupid scrape from the top of a van.

Anyhow, because the skin on my head was peeled back like a grape, they stitched me up at a local hospital and, believe it or not, I performed that very night with the San Diego Symphony! I swear if I ever go bald—and my hairline IS rising a bit every year—my scarred-up head will make me look like I just escaped from prison. 🎤

CHAPTER 6

Bob Hamilton taught me more about music and life itself in just two years than one might imagine.

I see myself singing in Sweden at the Gothenburg Opera House with my Frankford High School award-winning Ambassadors of Song choir and many years later singing on that same stage with the Oak Ridge Boys. Our choir was named one of the best in America by music educators, and we proceeded to raise enough money for a tour to Scandinavia in my junior year of high school, and it was a tremendous education for me.

One of the great influencers in my life was our choir director Robert G. Hamilton, who would go on to direct the famed Philadelphia Boys Choir until his retirement. Bob Hamilton taught me more about music and life itself in just two years than one might imagine.

I have written often about my crossroads theory—where God places certain people in your pathway over the course of your lifetime. If you are paying attention and your mind and heart are open, you will bond with that person—and because of him or her, you will become influenced to take the right road until the next person appears at the next needed moment.

Bob Hamilton met me at one of my biggest crossroads when I realized that I wasn't smart enough to become a veterinarian—and too poor to ever go to college anyway—and that music would become my pathway. I was also in that transition period between being a street rat and a new Christian, plus my daddy just had a stroke. Mister H was like a father to me, and how I needed him at the time.

CHAPTER 7

If we can start generating hit records to go with that energetic stage show, the sky is the limit for the Oak Ridge Boys.

I see myself and my singing partners meeting our manager, Jim Halsey, for the first time in Tonawanda, New York. Out of the clear blue sky, Jim's powerful booking agency called our office to see if we could fill in for a canceled act for shows in Rhode Island opening for Mel Tillis and on to Tonawanda, New York, to open up for Roy Clark.

Jim heard we tore up Warwick, Rhode Island, from Mel when he called Jim to say, "You had better check these guys out! They are hot!"

So Jim came to Tonawanda the next night and saw us hit the stage singing only gospel songs and pretty much destroying the place. My life, and the lives of all the Oaks, was again at a crossroads. This time God placed Jim Halsey in our path, and he became our manager, friend, and spiritual advisor right up to this very day. We call him our godfather, and I cannot imagine where we would be without him.

We gathered in a circle with Jim after we came off stage, and he told us things that have become part of music folklore.

"First off, you need to quit trying not to offend your old gospel fans and get off that fence and start adding country songs to your set. Next, we need to start booking shows so you can start making a living and I can get important promoters and fair buyers out to see you.

"We need to get you with a record label and a producer who can do right by you, because after seeing you guys onstage, I can tell you that you are just three minutes away (meaning a hit record!) from being the biggest act in the business.

"If we can start generating hit records to go with that energetic stage show, the sky is the limit for the Oak Ridge Boys. There is not a lot of pure energy in the country field right now, and you guys ARE pure energy."

Then he asked us to all hold hands, and he proceeded to lead us in a word of prayer asking God to watch over us and to guide our decisions. He still does that to this very day.

As of this writing [in 2021 at the time], our godfather is now over ninety years old and is as vibrant and creative as ever. You can read more about Jim Halsey in my book *On the Road with The Oak Ridge Boys* or in his own book *Star Maker: How to Make It in the Music Business*.

I'll tell you this much, without our godfather our pathway forward would have been entirely different—if at all.

CHAPTER 8

"Now here is little Joey Bonsall to favor us with a selection."

I see myself singing "What a Day That Will Be" in my church and later in a talent contest in Harrisburg, Pennsylvania, which I lost! I see a girl from Calvary Church named Ruth Burris playing piano for me.

My mom taught me a lot of old gospel and country songs when I was little, and I sang solos in church quite often.

"Now here is little Joey Bonsall to favor us with a selection."

And my selection would be "The Glory Land Way," "Dust on the Bible," or any one of Elvis's songs from the *His Hand in Mine* album, which I played every single day. I loved hearing the Jordanaires adding their four-part harmony to Elvis's gospel songs as well as the big hits. They also backed Ricky Nelson on many of his hits. I didn't realize it at the time, but the four-part harmony of the Jordanaires influenced me greatly when I was just a little kid listening to those old records in my bedroom.

CHAPTER 9

Trying hard not to laugh, I reached for the blood of Christ,
which was actually little bitty glasses of Welch's grape juice.

I see myself singing with my first quartet, the Faith Four. I see us rehearsing in my basement, while I am learning to play enough chords to get us by upon a dilapidated upright piano my mom bought for me. How they ever got that thing down there is still a mystery to me.

I see my basement office right by the furnace where I would call preacher after preacher all over the East Coast and try to talk them into letting our little group come and sing in their church for a love offering. Many would book us . . . many would not. Many would provide enough offering to pay our expenses ... many would not.

My sister, Nancy, who has always had a beautiful voice, sang with me in the Faith Four for a while. She was just thirteen years old at the time and used to wow a church audience with her amazing voice.

One time though, we were singing at a morning service for a church in Scranton, Pennsylvania, and they called all of us forward for Communion. Well, me and Nancy were kneeling together when the bread went by. The bread was little pieces of crackers representing the body of Christ, and they were stale and terrible tasting.

Trying hard not to laugh, I reached for the blood of Christ, which were little bitty glasses of Welch's grape juice, and I downed mine right off to get that awful cracker taste out of my mouth. I then reached for another one, but you really don't GET another one, and it struck my sister so funny she began to laugh uncontrollably.

Well, I started shaking and laughing as well. We had our heads buried in the altar when the preacher came down and placed his hands upon our heads and yelled out to the congregation:

"Everyone stand and pray for these blessed young singers as they are rejoicing in the Spirit!"

That made us laugh even harder. We were trembling as the people prayed louder and louder. We just raised our hands in the air and our eyes were filled with tears from laughing so hard we kind of pulled it all off—kind of! The Faith Four was afraid to ever return to that church again.

CHAPTER 10

G.I. Joe and Lillie

I see myself writing the book of a lifetime!
You will read a lot about my parents in many of the
chapters in *I See Myself.* But in 2003, I wrote a very deep
reflection of their lives in the best-selling *G.I. Joe and Lillie:
Remembering a Life of Love and Loyalty.* Not many folks get to
honor their parents in such a way, and I thought I'd share with
you how the whole thing came about.

It started with a song.

I don't write many songs, as I seem to prefer the written
word, but I wrote the song "G.I. Joe and Lillie" long before
there was even a glimmer of a book idea. One night just for
fun I wrote a short story based upon the song about how my
father was a hero of D-Day and beyond, met my Women's Army
Corps mother when the war ended, married, moved to Philadelphia, and gave birth to your author. After a piece of shrapnel
lodged in his carotid artery at age thirty-nine, his brain was permanently damaged, and the book sheds light on the amazing
love of a woman of faith who raised a family and stood by her
husband until the end.

In the meantime, the Oaks recorded my song as part of the
album *Colors,* and an idea was then pitched as a gift book with
a compact disc of the song included that, perhaps, might find

a point of sale by supermarket check-out lines. My book agent
Kathy Harris pitched the idea to a Christian book company
called New Leaf Press and an amazing thing happened. They
thought the short story was worthy enough to be turned into a
big book!

By then my parents had passed. And my mom had always
asked me if I would write a book about her and Daddy one day,
and I always promised her I would, so it seemed to me that God
was leading the way.

I told the publisher, "Yes. I can give you a book!"

So, for some more backstory, the governor of Tennessee at
the time, Don Sundquist, invited the four Oak Ridge Boys and
our wives to a private dinner at the Governor's Mansion. The
only other guest that night was the Tennessee prisons director,
and I was fortunate enough to sit by him. It turned out he was
quite a historian, and he asked me about my parents so I started
to tell him all about my dad and how he would hardly ever talk
about the war.

He suggested I read a book by author Stephen Ambrose
called *Citizen Soldiers*. He told me Ambrose had a unique way
of getting World War II veterans to talk and, if I read his book, I
would find out more about just what my dad and men like him
did in the war and would, perhaps, provide some insight on how
to approach my own project.

About a week later the book came in the mail, and I read it
all in one day. I love the work of Stephen Ambrose, so I bought
all of his books and read each with enthusiasm (especially *Band
of Brothers*). When it came time to work on my own book, I
now had a wealth of knowledge about young boys and their
experience in combat.

Then, I collected every bit of material I could find on D-Day
and the "Tough Ombres" of the 90th Infantry Division, which

my father's 359th Regiment was a part of. I was also able to gather many of my father's war records, and my sister found a lot of handwritten notes my mother had written about her time in the Women's Army Corps and the early days of their marriage after the war.

After I read Stephen Ambrose's books about D-Day and Dwight David Eisenhower, I felt prepared to start writing *G.I. Joe and Lillie.* I put everything in a big road case I called "Mommy and Daddy in a Bag." It included all the gathered material and even a bunch of photos.

I would take it to my hotel room while on tour, lay it all out on the bed, fire up the laptop, and every day I would try to write a chapter. I would write in a third-person style as their son Joey. By doing so, the reader wouldn't find out until the end that the son was also the author.

It really didn't matter if you knew that going in, but it was a good way to approach the writing, as it gave me the chance to rise up and look down upon the story line from a different point of view. And it was also a nice surprise for the reader to find out these two wonderful people were indeed my own parents.

Do you remember the movie *Field of Dreams* when the protagonist was able to meet his father at a young age "before the years got to him"? Well, utilizing this style, I was able to go back and meet both of my parents at a very young age. It was a very cool experience to write about them from that perspective.

It was also important to me that I got every detail right about World War II, D-Day, and the exploits of the 90th. I didn't want some old veteran one day to read my book and say, "Boy, that guy got it all wrong!" So many folks had lived the exact same life my parents had in those days of war and sacrifice, and many old veterans would read the book, and I really wanted them to say, "This guy got it right!"

Through the years I have heard from so many wonderful veterans who shed tears over my book. And it meant the world to me.

The old soldier and the woman who loved him is as old as time itself. The price paid and the sacrifice made is a story worth telling again and again, because this is what America is all about. These men and women, like my parents, were called the Greatest Generation for a reason. They went way beyond themselves and did extraordinary things to preserve the freedoms we all enjoy today. As the son of two veterans, that love of God, flag, and country has been instilled in my heart since I was a little boy.

G.I. Joe and Lillie . . . a song and a book. I kept my promise, Mom.

G.I. Joe and Lillie

He was a streetwise kid from Philly
Just nineteen in '44
Joined up in Uncle's army
Hit the beach and fought a war
A decorated hero
He never talks about those days
Because of guys like G.I. Joe our country's free today

She was Women's Army Corps
Raised in Carolina dirt
Escorting wounded young men home
From a burning hell on earth
The first time that she saw him
He was broken and alone
Lillie fell in love that day
When he winked and said hello

And Lillie sang this song to G.I. Joe

Let me hold you in my arms, handsome soldier
Take my hand for we are going home today
Let me kiss away your tears
Let me pray away your fears
I'll stay here with you
Till they carry us away

They married in the spring
All dressed up in army green
Took out a loan, bought a home
Raised a family
The war returned to G.I. Joe in 1965
The old wounds came back to haunt him
But Lillie's love kept him alive

Now they're living in a veteran's home
They've both grown old and gray
The medals earned so long ago
Now hang there in a case
Sometimes she finds him weeping
As he lay there in his bed
The distant sounds of battle
Still echo in his head

And Lillie sings this song to G.I. Joe

Let me hold you in my arms, handsome soldier
Take my hand for we are going home today
Let me kiss away your tears
Let me pray away your fears
I'll stay here with you
Till they carry us away

Someday they'll rest in Arlington
'Neath the red, the white, the blue
Safe in the arms of Jesus
When their journey here is through
An American love story
Not unlike a lot of others
Except that G.I. Joe and Lillie
Is my father and my mother*

---

* Written by Joe Bonsall, B's in the Trees Music, administered by Capitol CMG

CHAPTER 11

Mom wouldn't let me drive to school ever again.

I see myself wrecking my dad's old 1959 Ford station wagon I inherited after his stroke and then wrecking my 1959 Chevrolet winged monster as well. The first accident was entirely my fault as I left the Frankford High School campus and drove to the new McDonalds for lunch. As I sped back to school, I ran a stop sign I honestly never saw and got hit broadside.

To this day I have never forgotten the corner of Devereaux and Battersby. They rushed me to the hospital and stitched me up, and I think I learned a lesson. Mom wouldn't let me drive to school ever again, but she eventually helped me buy the '59 Impala.

I really loved that car despite the fact that on a highway the wind would get under the back wings and lift you up a bit. I guess, in retrospect, it wasn't a very good design, but I still loved it.

I was stopped at a red light when a drunk driver slammed into me. My white winged monster was totaled, and once again for me . . . more stitches!

CHAPTER 12

I guess I was singing to myself instead of paying attention.

I see my myself working as a veterinarian's assistant, a short order cook, a mail-boy for a tool company, and a sales order clerk for Jack Frost Cane Sugar. I can easily visualize the Faith Four Dodge van, that my mom also signed for, dropping me off in downtown Philly early on a Monday morning for work after singing all weekend long at a Christian campground or a church somewhere on the East Coast.

That red Dodge van had "THE FAITH FOUR QUARTET Representing America's Christian Youth" emblazoned on the side. Nobody in downtown Philly understood the significance at all when it would pull up at 5th and Market and let me out so I could head on up to the Jack Frost Sugar offices on the third floor of the Rohm and Haas building, change clothes in the bathroom, and head to my desk in the sales order department, where I would take sugar orders all day long and then hand them over to the transportation department for delivery.

Although my job was fast-paced and fun, and there were pretty girls all over the place, it sure wasn't like singing. I'll admit, the Faith Four weren't really all that good, but I day-dreamed at my desk all day, every day about music.

I got called out one day for sending a truckload of sugar to an Acme market warehouse in north Philly instead of a Grand

Union market warehouse in New Jersey. It might have even been a truckload of molasses. I guess I was singing to myself instead of paying attention.

Thankfully they didn't fire me.

CHAPTER 13

We called ourselves "The GristleAirs"—all gristle, all of the time, 24/7 . . . GRISTLE!

I see myself singing every night with the Oak Ridge Boys to a sold-out arena with lasers and smoke and the first computerized lighting system ever used for a country music show. I see myself singing "Dancin' the Night Away," "Elvira," and "Bobbie Sue" while running around on the various ramps built just for me to run around on.

In younger days nobody brought as much energy to the stage as we did. We have never taken one ticket buyer for granted. If people were willing to take several hours out of their lives and spend their hard-earned money to come out and hear us sing, well, we have always felt that they deserved the very best we had to give on every song and every show.

We have always felt that way, and I believe that is one good reason why the Oak Ridge Boys are still around. We may not play the big arenas anymore, but we still play lots of smaller arenas, theaters, and performance centers from coast to coast as well as many casinos, state and county fairs, and quite a few music festivals. And singing today is just as exciting as it was in what I always refer to as "The Heydays," because in those days we were as hot as a band could be. And secretly, we called ourselves "The GristleAirs"—all gristle, all of the time, 24/7 . . . GRISTLE!

CHAPTER 14

I can live without singing . . . I can NOT live without my Mary.

I see myself meeting Mary for the first time at a show in Freeport, Illinois. All she did was smile at me and an alarm went off deep inside of my soul indicating I might never be able to live without this woman, which proved to be oh so true. I am thankful I see her sweet smile every single day. She has become my rock in this crazy world.

Just recently I had a wooden plaque engraved with the words, "I can live without singing . . . I can NOT live without my Mary." It has been true since that night in 1978, our marriage in 1982, right up to this present day.

Many never find true love or a real soul mate like in the movies, but I was fortunate to do so. We promised each other long ago we would grow old together and so far, we seem to be pulling it off.

What is love? When you stare deep into her eyes over a candlelight dinner and an overwhelming feeling tells your heart and soul that perhaps you have known this woman since the very beginning of time and there is absolutely no way you can go any farther without her!

Joe and Mary . . . legendary. 🎤

CHAPTER 15

I see the guys arriving with flowers and pink cigars to celebrate the birth of my daughter.

I see myself watching my Oak Ridge Boy brothers putting every bit of money they had on a bed in a hotel room in our struggling days so I could afford to fly from Montana to Nashville to see the birth of my daughter Jennifer. I see myself at a hospital seeing my first wife, Barbara, going through so much pain, yet such a reward was manifested in that miracle of life.

Jen is all grown up and living in Florida now and married to a great husband, who once told me he would be strong and true and look after my daughter to the end of time. Dan Stevens has been a man of his word over all these years, and I love him dearly.

Barbara and I were married for thirteen years before we both decided we couldn't make it work anymore. I take much of the blame for this, because these were crazy years in my life and quite frankly, she didn't really want to be a part of my musical escapades anymore. She was and is a good woman though, and she has done just fine without a wandering minstrel in her life.

I see myself flying back to Montana after Jennifer was born and waiting on the Oaks' tour bus to arrive and pick me back up at a Holiday Inn before rolling on to Western Canada. I see the guys arriving with flowers and pink cigars to celebrate the birth of my daughter.

Jennifer was a light in my life when she was born, and her light still shines brightly today! I joined the Oak Ridge Boys in October 1973 at the ripe old age of twenty-five. I moved in with Duane Allen and his wife, Norah Lee, until early January of 1974, when I could move my pregnant wife and the few possessions we owned from Buffalo to Hendersonville, Tennessee. I have always been grateful to DA and NL for allowing me to live in their home during this time of adjustment.

Jennifer was born on March 3.

CHAPTER 16

Nobody was seriously hurt but . . .

I see myself in the passenger seat of a Buick on the Pennsylvania Turnpike with the Faith Four quartet as the car lost control in a light rain and skidded into several other cars and then crashed into a guardrail. Nobody was seriously hurt, but what a nightmare it was for a bunch of young quartet singers.

It took a long time for me to get over that one.

CHAPTER 17

I wasn't tough enough to be a policeman, so I just kept on singing.

I see myself at a Chevy Dealership on Frankford Avenue watching my dear, supportive mother once again signing her name for a brand-new, used 1963 Impala convertible I would also wreck, but not totally. I did have the car painted red at the body shop instead of the battleship gray beforehand.

I see myself sleeping and living in that same car in Buffalo, New York, for an entire summer while singing with the Keystones. That winter the Mancini family took me into their home, as there was no sleeping in a car during a Niagara Frontier winter. It could drop three feet of lake-effect snow overnight along Lake Ontario, and it was always so damp and cold up there. I think I fought a cold all the time in those days, so I was happy to move in with the Mancinis.

I see myself eating the best Italian food ever prepared by Fran Mancini, and I see Lieutenant Danny Mancini trying to talk me into being a Buffalo policeman and quit trying to make a living singing. He would make sure I got into the Police Academy and help me out all he could.

His heart was pure, and his motives were meaningful, but I wasn't tough enough to be a policeman, so I just kept on singing. The Mancinis were like family to me and were placed at the crossroad just when I needed them. And besides that, Fran's lasagna and Danny's homemade red wine were quite incredible. Dan and Fran . . . thank you!

CHAPTER 18

"I only hope that all those things you believed would happen after death are happening for you now."

I see myself as a friend of John R. Cash and recording late night gospel songs with him at his House of Cash recording studio during a time when we were opening shows for him. I see June Carter Cash cooking dinner for us and always referring to us as her babies.

I see myself singing the Bill Gaither–penned "Loving God, Loving Each Other" at her funeral in 2003 as an old Johnny Cash looked up at us and mouthed the words, *"Thank you."*

We also sang at Momma Maybelle Carter's funeral many years before at John and June's request. We sang a song that John loved called "That's Just Like Jesus," written by Garland Craft, a longtime friend who played piano for the Keystones as well as the Oak Ridge Boys and is a masterful songwriter. We would later record that song with Johnny.

I see myself at the movie theater watching the biopic *Walk the Line* and then visiting John and June's resting place after and placing a rose on their tombstones. I remember, after John passed, a relative looked down into his casket and said, "I only hope that all those things you believed would happen after death are happening for you now."

I assure you, all those things were and ARE happening for Johnny Cash as well as June Carter. 🎤

CHAPTER 19

"Here she comes, Joey."

I see myself driving Daddy and Mommy to Veterans Hospitals in Coatesville, Pennsylvania, Wilmington, Delaware, and East Orange, New Jersey, where they told us Daddy had been rehabilitated as far as he would ever be and he would be disabled for the rest of his life.

I see his funeral in Macungie, Pennsylvania, and his burial at Arlington National Cemetery around thirty-six years after his debilitating stroke. I see my mommy at his graveside knowing she would later join him there in the sacred ground. And she would, indeed, be laid to rest with Daddy just nine months later.

I see myself on that day in the Arlington parking lot with my sister, Nancy, and my daughter Jennifer, waiting for her body to arrive. My sister whispered, "Here she comes, Joey" as a blue hearse pulled up beside us. Then, just like Daddy before, the soldiers of the old guard carried her flag-draped coffin and honored her with a 21-gun salute and "Taps" as her body rested in a silver coffin all wrapped up in an Oak Ridge Boys blanket.

I had seen Daddy's remains but never saw my mother's, and I did not want to. I'll see her again in God's time, and she will be forever young and beautiful.

Diabetes took my mom. Just one week before she passed, I visited her in what she called the "Soldiers Home." She asked if

I would sing to her. I held her hand and sang her favorite Oak Ridge Boys song, "I Guess It Never Hurts to Hurt Sometimes."

I so loved and adored my precious mother. Read more about her in my book *G.I. Joe and Lillie.* I promise you will love her as well.

CHAPTER 20

Thank you, Mr. President.

I see myself sitting on the deck at Walker's Point in Kennebunkport, Maine, drinking morning coffee with a former president, philosophizing over every single topic one might imagine. I see us fishing many times off the Maine Coast for bluefish in a presidential craft, while a Secret Service vessel tried hard to keep up.

I see all the Oaks and our wives living out one amazing adventure after another because of George and Barbara Bush. We even spent the night in the White House once after a command performance in the East Room.

So many memories. I see my Mary crying because she couldn't believe that a little small-town Illinois girl was sleeping in the Queens' Bedroom. Thank you, Mr. President.

I see myself along with Duane Allen, William Golden, and Richard Sterban singing "Amazing Grace" at his funeral because we had once promised him that we would.

I have stayed far away from politics in this book. Our friendship with George H. W. Bush over the years transcended politics and has been chronicled in at least fourteen books that I know of. I will just say again that our relationship with George and Barbara over many decades made us better Americans, and I deeply miss them both. 🎤

CHAPTER 21

Oh, to sing in a big-sounding, power harmony quartet and travel in a big tour bus.

I see myself riding in a very cool white Buick convertible that belonged to a youth leader named Bunkie Smulling. The car was always jam-packed with Christian Endeavor kids who one day talked me into driving with them to the Philly suburb of Ardmore to hear my first ever gospel quartet concert at the high school auditorium. They had tried in vain for years to get me to hang out with them instead of wasting my life sitting on a corner with hoodlums, and I would just ignore them or shoo them away. But I really did want to ride in that car.

One could say that Bunkie and these Christian kids also appeared at a crossroads because I sure did need the change in my life that only faith in Jesus Christ could bring.

I see myself in that auditorium being mesmerized by the Blackwood Brothers, with J. D. Sumner singing amazing bass, and never realizing what a dear friend and mentor he would turn out to be over the years ahead.

I see the Couriers looking cool and singing cool, and I realized at that very moment on that very evening that THIS was what I wanted to do. I wanted to sing like those guys were singing. Oh, to sing in a big-sounding, power harmony quartet and travel in a big tour bus. I once flunked geometry and had to go

41

to summer school to make it up because, instead of drawing circles and trapezoids, I was drawing pictures of tour buses and stage plots.

As a side note, the Couriers also became dear friends. Their examples, and their Christian witness, meant the world to me. I never realized on that night in Ardmore, Pennsylvania, how much these men would influence my life. Even today if a Couriers song shuffles by in my music library, it always brings a memory and a few tears. God placed these men at the crossroads, along with Bunkie and those Christian Endeavor kids, who never gave up on me! 🎤

CHAPTER 22

"Turn Your Eyes upon Jesus"

I see myself at a Christian Endeavor youth camp in South Jersey accepting Jesus Christ as my personal Savior around a campfire, while about a hundred or so other kids sang "Turn Your Eyes upon Jesus." I see my life immediately changing from being a street urchin wannabe hoodlum into a gospel music–singing witness for Jesus.

I see the things of earth growing strangely dim in the light of His glory and grace as all my mother's prayers began to come true. As I wrote in the book *G.I. Joe and Lillie*, it is hard to be scared when you can hear your mother on her knees by her bed praying for you.

As a side note, I spent some great times at summer camps when I was growing up. When I was just nine years old, I went to a YMCA camp in the Pocono Mountains. The kids there were pretty rough, but I so enjoyed being out in the woods and learning about nature. Later, my sister, Nancy, and I both attended a camp called Paradise Farms, which was a lot of fun since it got us away from the concrete in Kensington. However, that Christian Endeavor Camp Ockanickon in Medford, New Jersey—now a YMCA Camp—changed my life forever.

CHAPTER 23

Joseph Sloan Bonsall Senior never saw himself as a hero, but this is my book and I say that my daddy WAS a hero.

I see myself as a kid watching my father having nightmares about the war. I hear my sister crying while my mom would cradle and console him as he knelt on the floor of the upstairs hallway of our little row house. That was long before a piece of shrapnel lodged in his carotid artery and changed our lives.

I see myself many years later playing seven-card stud poker with him on our old kitchen table on Jasper Street. Many times when the Oak Ridge Boys played a show somewhere in the Northeast, if it was at all possible, I would figure out a way to visit my parents. Daddy and I would sometimes play cards all night long. We started with pennies, quickly moved to silver, and within an hour or so we were playing with green. He was usually able to add quite a bit of cash from my jar to his jar on these visits.

Mom always kept our jars of cash hidden away until such a time as "Joey was coming home." In those days he was wheel-chair-bound, his right arm was dead, and he could only say a few words. But I was able to understand him just fine when he would begin to cry and talk about the war as his straight flush beat my full house. And another five dollars or so changed jars.

44

I see myself visiting him and Mommy years later at the Southeastern Pennsylvania Veterans Center, where they both lived out the remainder of their days. He was old and tired at that point and didn't even care about playing poker anymore. He just wanted to die and did so at age seventy-six seeming somehow much older than his years.

I see myself staring down at what was left of him in a casket and a day later I see him lowered into the sacred ground of Arlington National Cemetery as a flag was presented to my mother from a grateful nation, while guns fired and "Taps" played. I see myself more torn up about his death than I ever thought I'd be.

I see myself writing about him in my book *G.I. Joe and Lillie* and crying tears as I wrote. The man was a hero of the first wave of attack on D-Day at the ripe old age of nineteen. He fought hand-to-hand in the brutal Hedgerow battles, and on D-Day, he and fifty of his Tough Ombres of the 90th Infantry fought the bloody battle of Saint-Lô, France, where he got hit hard while taking out Nazi machine gun nests all by himself.

He was shot in the back, his behind, and all down his leg and foot where he lost a toe and part of his heel. And his body would regurgitate shrapnel until his last days on earth.

He worked hard in factories as an electrician. He drank too much, loved his wife and kids, could swim like Johnny Weissmuller, execute a perfect jackknife off the highest dive platform at Cedar Lake Park in Jersey, fix any machine in any factory, climb a ladder like a cat, loved to boo the Philadelphia Phillies, and still had time to help save the world.

He had a debilitating stroke at age thirty-nine, and he cried a lot. There is something between a son and his father that cannot be explained. We butted heads often. I thought he never understood me. He taught me to shave. He took me to see the

Phillies and the Eagles. He called me useless because I couldn't hammer a nail in straight (I still can't) or couldn't find his needle-nosed pliers in his tool pouch when he needed them.

He also assured me I would never go to war—he would make certain of it. And he did just that by having a stroke and leaving me as sole support of my little family ship.

I never saw Viet Nam because of Joseph Sloan Bonsall Sr., who never saw himself as a hero, but this is my book and I say that my daddy WAS a hero. When I was little and became afraid of one dark thought or another, I would always close my eyes and picture Daddy's face and my fears would subside.

Daddy was a soldier. Daddy fought the Nazis. Daddy protected and took care of us. And God knows he did until the day he needed more care than he was able to give.

I see myself thinking about him every single day.

CHAPTER 24

I knew that Richard Sterban may have been the only other guy in Philadelphia, or even South Jersey, who shared my deep love for quartet singing.

I see myself following Richard Sterban all around a Gimbels department store in Northeast Philly in the men's clothing department where he worked. I had heard him sing bass, and I knew that he may have been the only other guy in Philadelphia, or even South Jersey, who shared my deep love for quartet singing. I even started going to a voice teacher named Aunt Betty because Richard went there.

I see myself answering the phone one night with Richard on the line inviting me to join the Keystone Quartet and sing full-time. I see myself leaving my job at the sugar company and moving to Harrisburg, Pennsylvania, where I would sing and starve to death for a quite a few years thereafter. But I was singing with Richard!

I see the Keystones moving to Buffalo, New York, where we would promote gospel concerts all over western New York and Pennsylvania and Ontario, Canada.

I see Richard leaving us for Nashville to join the Stamps Quartet and tour with Elvis. I see Richard joining the Oak Ridge Boys in 1972, just one year before I would join and once again reunite with him.

We are old guys now, but we are still the best of friends. As a side note, I was still living on the Niagara Frontier and singing with the Keystones when the Elvis tour came to Buffalo. Richard provided tickets for the show, and we even had dinner together that night.

I was thrilled to see one of my childhood heroes in concert for the first time. But was even more thrilled to hear the King introduce Richard on the stage of what we called The Aud back then. I thought about that night when, years later, the Oak Ridge Boys played the very same Aud with Kenny Rogers and later our own arena tour. The Aud is gone now but, oh the memories.

CHAPTER 25

We never gave up . . . Johnny Cash was right . . . as usual!

I see myself listening to the Oak Ridge Boys singing on the radio for the first time realizing that I may be able to start making a living at this singing thing. "Y'all Come Back Saloon" became our first big country hit and set the peg for many awards and hit records to come.

I see myself heading to the stage to win our first Country Music Association Vocal Group of the Year award and, instead of heading to the podium to receive our award, we ran to the host of the show and group-hugged him.

Johnny Cash whispered, "I told you so," and indeed he had in a hotel room in Las Vegas years before. He had said, "Someday the world will know what I know and that is the Oak Ridge Boys are magic. All one has to do is stand here in the midst of you or hear you sing to know this. I know you guys are struggling right now, but you can't give up or the world will never know what I know now!"

We never gave up . . . Johnny Cash was right . . . as usual!

🖋

CHAPTER 26

I limped off the football field, scratched my name off the list, and joined the choir instead. I have been singing ever since.

I see myself playing football for the Lighthouse Boys Club Lions. As a 125-pound wide receiver, I see myself catching a football from quarterback Bobby Devlin (I can't believe I remember Bobby) and scoring a touchdown. Our team was a ragtag poor bunch as we didn't even have uniforms alike. Only our matching white helmets indicated we were a team at all. But the Holmesburg Astronauts—a suburban team who were all dressed out like the freakin' Pittsburgh Steelers—was our opponent that day, and they were mean as sewer rats.

After I was tackled in the endzone, their whole team piled on top of me and wouldn't get off. One guy was punching me in the ribs. I have always been claustrophobic, and I was really freaking out under there.

Suddenly, my mother comes flying out of the stands and starts to rip Astronauts off me two at time. I couldn't believe what I was hearing. Was that my mom yelling, "Get off of him, you little bastards!"?

Was I embarrassed? Perhaps a little. But boy, was I loving my mother. I thought I was a pretty good football player though as I played free safety and wide receiver for various Pop Warner League teams, but then I arrived at Frankford High School . . .

50

I see myself getting absolutely killed trying to make the football team. Frankford was always a high school football powerhouse and, in fact, they won the city championship two out of the three years I was there.

At tryouts they had to weed out kids quickly, and I just didn't have the meat on my bones to take hits from a kid who weighed 200-plus, so I limped off the field, scratched my name off the list, and joined the choir instead.

I have been singing ever since. As a side note, over the past few years I have become friends and brothers with the current Frankford High School football coach Bill Sytsma, an inspiring man and a bright light to kids growing up in a tougher-than-ever city. Coach Sytsma loves me, but I still don't think he would let me play. ✒

CHAPTER 27

We were a mix of Protestants, Catholics, Hebrews, black kids, white kids, Germans, Polish, Italians, and several Heinz 57 mashups like me who would have done anything for one another.

I see myself leading all the other boys in the neighborhood. If Joey went left, Freddie and Jimmy and Charlie and Johnny and Paul and Herbie and Harvey went left. If Joey went right, well, you know.

There were about a dozen boys who grew up together in the Kensington section of North Philadelphia on streets named Jasper, Emerald, Clearance, Tioga, Atlantic, and Venango, and we were really a unique and very diverse little bunch.

We were a mix of Protestants, Catholics, Hebrews, black kids, white kids, Germans, Polish, Italians, and several Heinz 57 mashups like me who would have done anything for one another. A melting pot of young boys who actually melted and were always together playing baseball, tackle football, two-hand touch, handball, wall ball, wire ball, stick ball, step ball, half ball, and many other made-up games.

You could also find us pitching or flipping baseball cards, going to the movies, invading Flannery's candy store or Everet's Cheesesteak and pizza shop, playing pinball or perhaps just sitting together upon any random corner steps in the neighborhood talking and laughing about the Phillies, girls, TV shows, girls, the Eagles, girls, rock and roll, or perhaps . . . GIRLS!

We called ourselves the Blackhawks, and we were a tough little bunch—*HAWK-AAAAAAAA!* I have always enjoyed being surrounded by a bunch of guys who had my back. Friends I could count on who would always be honest with me. Friends I could trust with my secrets, my money, my girlfriend, and my very life. Friends I would die for!

In a way, the Blackhawks of my youth would eventually metamorphose into the Faith Four, the Keystones, and finally the Oak Ridge Boys of today. Duane Allen, William Lee Golden, and Richard Sterban have become my little posse over all these decades. Partners whom I could trust with my life— who always told the truth and had my back right up until this very moment. Like present-day Blackhawks, I would die for any one of them—in a New York minute!

CHAPTER 28

How did HE ever wind up with the likes of HER?

I see myself being very unlucky with girls until eleventh grade when Joni Easton became my first love. Before Joni, I struck out with Linda Sidelsky, Susan Gehan, Sandra Cane, Jackie Van Matre, Linda D'Angelo, Janet Williamson, Donna Law, and even Nancy Hanstein, who dated every boy in the neighborhood but me.

But ah . . . Joni Easton found favor in Joey Bonsall. She was a beautiful blonde girl and she even loved to hear me sing. In my senior year at Frankford High all the other guys were envious of me as we walked down the halls hand in hand—the same as guys when they have seen me with my Mary over the years. I am certain guys were thinking, *How did HE ever wind up with the likes of HER?*

Joni loved the Beatles, Jesus, designer skirts, and mohair sweaters and, for a while there, she loved me too. I see myself once beating the daylights out of some guy named Eddie Kuhn who tried to come between us. I see Joni washing the blood off my nicely starched white shirt.

I see myself standing on a corner alone a few years later watching her and a former Marine and Viet Nam vet named Harry exit the Bethany Christian Church after her wedding and drive off far away from me and my music ambitions. I see her and Harry coming to an Oak Ridge Boys show in Valley Forge, Pennsylvania, many years thereafter. She came backstage and kissed me on the cheek and congratulated me for making it in music and for never giving up on my dreams. I never saw her again after that night.

Semper Fi and goodbye . . . I hope they have both done well over the years.

CHAPTER 29

When the call came from William Lee Golden to consider moving to Nashville and joining the Oak Ridge Boys, I nearly jumped through the phone.

I see myself in yet another highway mishap. This one was a terrible bus wreck that pretty much ended my career with the gospel singing Keystones of Kenmore, New York. One of our guys driving the Flexliner bus fell asleep and crashed into a parked semi on the Illinois/Wisconsin Line. There were a few broken bones and, thankfully, we all survived. But my heart was broken. I knew then that my days of trying to make this group succeed were over.

After Richard left, I could never find another bass singer. So I hired a band and we became more of a Jesus Rock group. Even though it was fun and we were quite good, when the call came from William Lee Golden to consider moving to Nashville and joining the Oak Ridge Boys, I nearly jumped through the phone.

As a side note, that Keystone Flexliner bus was purchased from J. D. Sumner of the Stamps Quartet. He originally sang with the Blackwood Brothers, whom I saw at my first big time quartet concert.

Yet another full-circle relationship. 🎤

CHAPTER 30

Have you ever heard 50,000 people singing "Elvira"?

I see myself on one big festival stage after another over the years rocking our butts off singing to the thousands upon thousands of people gathered on a hot summer night to hear us perform. I see myself sweating through my socks and feeling young and strong and running with the wind at my back.

Have you ever heard 50,000 people singing "Elvira"? It is quite unforgettable. The Oak Ridge Boys are still invited to play at many of these huge country music festivals from CMA Fest to Country Thunder, from Jamboree in the Hills to the WE Fest and from Country Fest to Coachella. We are not the headliners anymore but more of a legendary presence. It is always an honor to be invited. 🎤

CHAPTER 31

To have a loving partner in life is a great blessing.

I see myself and my little sister, Nancy, as small children playing our own made-up, make-believe games in the basement of 3517 Jasper Street. We were superheroes, Big Fox and Little Fox, and with wooden swords in our hand we saved the neighborhood and the world from evildoers everywhere.

I love my sister with all of my heart. She has always been a caring person with such a giving spirit that has always reminded me of our mother. My mom always prayed that one day Nancy would find someone to love the way I found my Mary, and she eventually did. Her husband Chuck is a darn good man. I think the world of him, and he does take good care of my sister, and she takes good care of him.

It is called true love, and I am certain that Mommy is happy in heaven knowing that both of her kids are doing just fine down here and that both of her kids have a true and loving companion. I feel so sorry sometimes for the many who are traveling alone through this world who have nobody they can truly lean on. To have a loving partner in life is a great blessing. I know that is certainly the case for your author, and I try to never take it for granted. 🎤

CHAPTER 32

I see the rain dripping off the bill of his Phillies cap into his cup of beer and appearing to be the happiest I ever remember him being.

I see myself at Connie Mack Stadium at 21st and Lehigh with my father on a Sunday afternoon sitting in the stands watching the Phillies play the Pirates or the Reds or the Cubs. Baseball heroes like Robin Roberts and Richie Ashburn and Johnny Callison were down there playing in bright red and white uniforms upon a brilliant green field with bright white lines, and I just loved every minute.

The sights and sounds of those little-boy moments have never left me. That is why I love baseball so much. Time stands still at a ball game no matter which team is down there playing. But my heart will always belong to the Philadelphia Phillies.

I see myself praying that Daddy didn't drink too many beers (especially during a Sunday double header) so that we might get his old '49 Studebaker or '52 Ford or '53 Chevy or whatever car he was driving at the time home safe and sound—especially with me riding shotgun!

Many years later I see myself pushing Daddy's wheelchair into the old Veterans Stadium for a World Series game in the autumn of 1993 that lasted well into the night in a light rain. I see the rain dripping off the bill of his Phillies cap into his cup of beer and Daddy appearing to be the happiest I ever remember him being in that precious moment.

As I was as a kid, I don't think he ever wanted that game to end, and it almost didn't. That World Series game between the Phillies and Blue Jays went down as the longest nine-inning game in World Series history, and it all went wrong when Phillies relief pitcher Mitch Williams's arm went south in the 9th. I heard he tried to shoot himself after the game but kept missing low and away. Ba-Dum!

CHAPTER 33

On that night, in that space and at that time, the earth shifted a bit on its axis, and my life was again changed forever.

I see myself meeting the Oak Ridge Boys for the first time and becoming friends with them. The Keystones opened for them at a gospel show in Wilmington, Delaware. We pulled our old General Motors 4104 model bus right up behind their beautiful Silver Eagle coach. We had to park with one side up on the sidewalk so that when the air leaked out of our air bags the bus would appear to sit level. We didn't want the Oaks to see our bus all off to the side, and we also didn't want them to see the oil all over the back end—so we cleaned all that up as well.

The Oak Ridge Boys were incredible that night. So cool and so cutting edge. They didn't just sing gospel like every other group. Their hair was a bit longer. They had a band with a rock and roll drummer and they sang great songs. I was mesmerized by them. In the years moving forward, we would become close friends.

Duane Allen would produce albums on my Keystones and teach me the value of always recording great songs. His leadership and friendship still mean the world to me today. I see myself having late-night phone conversations with William Lee Golden, whom I called Bill back then. He always encouraged me to not only dream, but to dream big, and then to follow those dreams. He always believed in me and my talents. He still does, and I am grateful for him.

It all started that night in Wilmington, Delaware, when a young starving quartet met the hottest group in southern gospel. On that night, in that space and at that time, the earth shifted a bit on its axis, and my life was again changed forever. I would go on to promote shows with the Oak Ridge Boys up north, and they would reciprocate and bring us south.

We would roll to Hendersonville, Tennessee, often and record in Duane Allen's basement studio. He started an entire record label just for the Keystones and produced ten of our best albums! Eventually two of those early Keystone boys—Richard Sterban and I—would end up making music history with Duane and William Lee for decades to come. God had a plan. I am thankful I was paying attention when these men appeared at the crossroads. 🎤

CHAPTER 34

Jimmy Dean was a big star and he loved me.

I see myself and my partners up late at night with the man we called the cowboy, Jimmy Dean. We toured with him off and on in the mid-seventies. After a show, he would try out different sausage recipes that he would cook up on a hot plate for us in a hotel room. This was long before Jimmy Dean Sausage was "a thing."

How we loved JD. He taught us a lot about big-time show business and . . . well, sausage! I see myself singing back-up vocals to "Big John" on many a stage over those years, and later he would call me quite often. He never even said hello; he would just start telling joke after joke and every one of them was hilarious—but I could never repeat anyone of them to my mother.

Once, while in a supermarket my phone rang, and the next thing I heard was Jimmy reciting the most hideous poem. Then he just hung up. I looked up and right there in front of me was a life-sized cardboard cutout of him encouraging everyone to purchase some Jimmy Dean Sausage!

I miss that old cowboy. He was a pioneer of early television, a masterful performer, a big star, and he loved me. 🎤

CHAPTER 35

I see a sign that read, The Very Ground Here Is Crying.

I see myself touring the Soviet Union with Roy Clark and stunning the communist audiences with our four-part harmony, Roy's guitar and banjo—and even his balalaika virtuoso. Banjo hero Buck Trent was also on that tour, and Soviet audiences would scream when they played "Dueling Banjos."

I also see people beating on the side of our bus in Leningrad screaming at us to go back to America and bring back some help for the oppressed behind the Iron Curtain. I see them being beaten bloody as our bus pulled away from the concert hall.

I see myself crying in Riga, Latvia, while visiting the remains of a Nazi concentration camp where only Jewish children were kept prisoner. Their blood was taken and sent to Nazi soldiers on the front lines. Thirty thousand children were murdered there by the Butcher of Riga—Eric Rothman—who I hope is burning in the pit of hell as I write.

I see a wall with these words written on it, *May There Always Be Mommy, May There Always Be Sunshine, May There Always Be Me.* I see Roy Clark dropping Clark Bars everywhere with tears in his eyes. I see a sign that read, *The Very Ground Here Is Crying.*

One doesn't forget stuff like that . . . EVER! 🎤

CHAPTER 36

"But I bought you a case of Diet Coke."

I see myself in my basement as a boy with a pencil and a composition notebook writing stories about baseball players and gunfighters. I see myself on a trip to visit my parents and discovering my mother had cleaned out the area behind the basement stairs—in so doing, she threw out my entire baseball card and marble collections as well as all of my early writings.

I remember her apologizing and saying, "But I bought you a case of Diet Coke."

That made everything fine, I guess, but I sure would love to have all that stuff today. Thank God she never threw out her own handwritten memoirs of her early days as a little girl running away from the farm in North Carolina at age fifteen and eventually joining the Women's Army Corps.

She also chronicled her early days of meeting and marrying my father. I have often said that I may have been able to write the book *G.I. Joe and Lillie* without her little memoirs, but having them sure gave me a glimpse of them as young people.

I may no longer have my own writings about a gunfighter from Rhode Island named Providence Joe who helped tame the Wild West or my baseball card collection—which may have put both daughters through college!—but I had Lillie. She was the best mom a son could ever have.

Funny thing though, she could never catch me and my sister when we were kids. We were always pulling jokes on her. She had this awful fake plant in the living room, and we would hide it on her. One time on a cold winter day we put the plant outside on the front steps and when she went out to retrieve it, we shut and locked the door on her.

"JoeyNancy (always one word), you let me in right now! I have to pee . . . I just peed, dang it. I will wait until you're asleep in your beds and kill you both!"

We laughed for years over that one. Lillie couldn't catch us, and she never killed us either, although there were times when we seriously might have deserved it. ✒

CHAPTER 37

I am now a part of Philadelphia music history.

I see myself and Richard being inducted into the Philadelphia Music Hall of Fame beside so many of my music heroes, like deejays Joe Niagara and Jerry Blavat, and the likes of everyone from Dick Clark to Hall and Oates and Chubby Checker, the Stylistics, and even Freddy "Boom Boom" Cannon.

I am now a part of Philadelphia music history. A street kid from Kensington, who performed concert after concert all alone in my childhood bedroom in front of a mirror using a dust mop and a small lampshade as a microphone, is now in the Philadelphia Music Hall of Fame.

This is still very hard to fathom. 🎤

CHAPTER 38

American Bandstand *was a hoot!*

I see myself standing in line at 69th and Market Streets with a neighbor girl named Cathy Stathius and hoping to get into *American Bandstand.* To jitterbug and twist or, perhaps, do the watusi on national television . . . and I see Dick Clark himself years later inviting me to write about it in a book about the 25th anniversary of *Bandstand.*

I see myself writing about getting into the old WFIL-TV studio on several occasions. But most times the line was cut off long before me and Cathy ever came close. So we would just buy a hoagie at Pop's and eat it on the way back home on the elevated train, what we called the El, which would eventually take us back to the Tioga Street exit about a block or so from our rowhouses on Jasper Street.

Miss Stathius and I made it into the *Bandstand* studio a few times, and there are several memories that really stick out to me. The studio was much smaller than it appeared on television, for one thing. And there were three huge TV cameras covering the dance floor. When a red light would blink, indicating the live camera was on, teenagers would break their necks trying to dance in front of that camera, and it was quite funny.

I was always dressed for the occasion in my Fabian sweater, tight dress pants, and Chubby Checker Twister red shoes with the little zippers on the side, and I always had my hair combed up into the highest pompadour I could muster with a cute little DA, or Duck's Ass, carefully coifed in the back. With Cathy in her poodle skirt and saddle shoes, we looked like we should have been in a sitcom. Once while a guy named Ray Peterson lip-synched his hit song, "Tell Laura I Love Her," all the girls pretended to weep. *American Bandstand* was a hoot! 🖊

CHAPTER 39

*Ron Chancey became known as the 5th Oak. Ron just knew
what to do with us.*

I see myself at Woodland Sound Studios in Nashville recording one hit record after another hit record, and one gold
or platinum album after another, year after year under the
producing genius of Ron Chancey, who became known as the
5th Oak. Ron just knew what to do with us.

With Jim Foglesong as head of MCA Records, and Jim
Halsey managing, and Kathy Gangwisch doing publicity, four
boys from Philadelphia, Pennsylvania; Camden, New Jersey;
Taylortown, Texas; and Brewton, Alabama—who as young boys
all just wanted to sing in a quartet one day—became a household name and achieved a legendary status we never dreamed
possible . . . Well, perhaps Golden did! 🎤

CHAPTER 40

You don't mess with the son of a Women's Army Corps WAC!

I see myself walking through Harrowgate Square across from my house after picking up some laundry from a young Chinese couple who Mommy liked to help, when a neighborhood bully and his two buddies I always tried to avoid jumped me. Two guys held me, while the head creep punched and kicked me. As a final insult they tore the shirt I had on, which was a favorite of mine, and then dumped all my mother's laundry into the mud.

I had a two-toned Adirondack baseball bat back in those days, and I see myself going home to get it. I went back to the park and found all three of them smoking behind a little storage shed in the middle of the square, and I took after the main creep with my bat, and as the other two ran off I proceeded to break quite a few ribs with my home run swing.

I guess I nearly killed him because blood from his punctured lungs was coming out of his mouth. And to be honest, I didn't care much.

A bit later the Creep's father was at our door threatening all kinds of stuff, and I see my mother picking up the same bat and swinging it at him, while telling him that if he or his son ever showed up at our house again, she would crush his skull with it. They never did.

You don't mess with the son of a Women's Army Corps WAC!

CHAPTER 41

I see myself being inducted into the Gospel Music Hall of Fame.

I see myself being inducted into the Gospel Music Hall of Fame for our lifelong contributions even though in our younger days we upset the mainstream with our long hair, our style of clothes, our rock band, and our cutting-edge songs. I believe as time went by, the Gospel Music Association realized we were just a bit ahead of our time, and that our accomplishments and constant dedication to our southern gospel roots were worthy of "the Hall."

I see us taking in with us every former living member of the Oak Ridge Boys, from the '40s through the early '70s, including Lon "Deacon" Freeman, who was the only living original member of the group from the mid-forties.

That young Philly boy blasting the Statesmen, the Blackwood Brothers, and the Couriers in his little backroom bedroom on his hi-fi stereo set was now in the Gospel Music Hall of Fame. Pretty mind-boggling, but so many more honors were waiting down the road.

As a side note, years later when Johnny Cash was inducted posthumously into the Gospel Music Hall, it was the Oak Ridge Boys who were there to induct him. His son, John Carter, received the medallion on Johnny's behalf. 🎤

CHAPTER 42

Mary was quite the swimmer, and I would look up many times to see her flippers paddling up ahead and leaving me way behind in the plankton.

I see myself in Bora Bora with my Mary in the middle of the night lying back on a deck that stretched way out over a beautiful lagoon, staring up at the Southern Cross, and making love until the sun came up. I see us on many vacations that we were blessed to take during our younger years. Aside from Bora Bora, our favorite spot was Caneel Bay in St. John, U.S. Virgin Islands.

I see us snorkeling in the bay and chasing big sea turtles. Mary was quite the swimmer, and I would look up many times to see her flippers paddling up ahead and leaving me way behind in the plankton.

I see myself with Mary cruising the Caribbean on several occasions on the four-mast schooner Wind Star. In the middle of the night the engines would shut down and only the wind in the sails would move us from one island to another. We felt like a couple of pirates as we lay side by side in the night enjoying each other and not wanting these moments to end. They haven't ever ended really because life is full of such memories for Mary and me. How nice it is to dig them up and relive those special moments. 🎤

CHAPTER 43

How I love my daughters.

I see myself on what we always call a Daddy Daughter night when me and my Jennifer and Sabrina will go to downtown Nashville together and eat as much sushi as one could possibly imagine and then drive out to our farm on the Kentucky-Tennessee line and just have fun together. How I love my daughters.

A bonus that came with Mary when we married was her daughter, Sabrina, who has given us two wonderful grandchildren: Breanne, who has given us a great-grandson, Noah Chance; and Luke, who at the time of this writing serves in the United States Navy.

I see myself watching these two daughters grow into intelligent and precious women, and then I have watched my grandchildren do the same. I see this as an amazing tribute to my wife, Mary, and how she has loved and guided them all throughout their lives. I have likewise tried to be a good example, and I believe I have been.

CHAPTER 44

If you do not share my love for cats, you might want to skip this part of the book and move on to the next . . .

I see myself loving cats! Lots of cats throughout the years. If you do not share my love for cats, you might want to skip this part of the book and move on to the next . . . When our Sabrina was just a little girl, she brought into our home the first cat I have ever known. He was a big orange tabby named Pumpkin, and I just loved that boy. I would make him a sage in my Molly the Cat book series.

The only cats I knew growing up in my old neighborhood in Philly were feral alley cats, and they were never very pleasant. But the Pumpkin kitty taught me early on that being around a cat could really be a great experience if you take the time to understand them.

As Mark Twain once wrote, "Having a cat always leads to having more cats," and multiple kitties have always been a part of our lives with each one bringing a certain individuality, love, and personality to our home.

Our second cat was a little Russian Blue named Yuri, who passed away at a very young age because of kidney failure. He was a sweet little spirit, who just adored Mary. To be honest, he didn't really like me very much, but, as I have learned over the years, my wife is a much better cat whisperer than I am. Most of the time I take second place, but I have never really minded the position. Yuri was a special little fellow for the time God allowed him to be with us.

Then there was our big girl, Gypsy Lee. One day we looked outside and there she was. She would not be the last cat someone dumped on our lawn, but she was the first. She was a black-and-white kitty who had half a moustache that was just funny.

Then the Oak Ridge Boys were playing in Omaha, Nebraska, for an entire week at an event called Aksarben (*Nebraska* spelled backwards), and Mary accompanied me on that trip. Well, one day we went to a mall pet shop and saw this little black-and-white tuxedo kitten who spoke to our hearts. We adopted him, naming him Omaha, of course, and he flew back to Nashville with us. I think often of our wonderful little Omi, who was the funniest little cat we ever had.

Our next feline arrival was brought to us by our nephew Gabe, who found the little kitten all alone and soaking wet from the rain and brought her to Mary. We named her Molly and made her famous in my Molly the Cat book series published by Ideals children's books, which were amazingly successful and established me as an author.

This series of four books—*Molly, The Home, Outside,* and *Brewster* (where a slobbering bulldog enters the fray)—were beautifully illustrated by Erin Marie Mauterer and featured our four cats—Molly, Pumpkin, Omi, and Gypsy.

But perhaps the best story of all was our Sally Ann kitty, who was here with us for almost twenty-three years. I wrote a wonderful and very moving story about her and how she came to be, and my publisher graciously allowed it to be added as a bonus story in the back of this book. I promise you will love Sally Ann!

Then there was our super model, Callie, who was an outdoor kitty that Mary rescued and brought into our home, vowing her little paws would never touch concrete ever again. She was part angora with long, beautiful calico-and-white fur, with a big plum of a tail, and a stunning face. She was really a beautiful girl. We would eventually lose her to cancer, but her paws never touched concrete ever again.

Ted was born on the front porch of a home out by our farm. He was part of the second litter born on that porch. We found homes for every cat in both litters, eventually captured mama cat and got her fixed, and took the little gray one home with us. Ted was the most destructive cat we ever had in his younger days and, to this day, after destroying some rather expensive collectibles, he is the only cat Mary thought about strangling. She would call him a hillbilly when another collectible hit the floor. But he mellowed with age, and we eventually lost Ted to cancer as well.

We received a call one day from our daughter Sabrina who was just so distraught that there was this orange cat out in the country whose fur was all matted, he was eaten up with ticks, and a bunch of good ol' boys were about to shoot him to put him out of his misery. I remember Mary answering in her firmest voice, "You bring that cat to me right now," and that is just what Sabrina did.

We took him to the vet and got him shaved and fixed up, named him Sunny, and he lived with us for fifteen years before he passed. He was a handsome cat, longhaired and part Maine coon, we thought, and we sure hated to see him go.

One day a neighbor called and said she saw a kitten hanging around a drain outside of our house. Someone had once again dumped a little girl kitten we took in, of course, and named her Baybé. We meant to find a home for her, but after an exam it was discovered she had a hole in her heart and might not live very long, so we didn't want to give away a defective kitten and we kept her. After a trip to the University of Tennessee Veterinary Center, they informed us she could live a long life with her heart defect, and she did just that. Baybé passed at the age of eighteen in 2021. She was a sweet kitty and, as Mary says, "There was never a bad bone in her body!"

During most of this time, we had two outdoor cats who decided to live with us. They came to us one day and just stayed. Blackie and Bud both guarded the perimeter, they both came inside from time to time, they were both loved, fed, and looked after by Mary. They both passed away at the early age of ten years old and both died of congestive heart failure. I still look outside sometimes and expect to see them out there somewhere, perhaps chasing birds or helping Mary in the garden, or just lounging on a deck chair. They were both real characters, and I miss them. Bud and Blackie . . . rest in peace, guys.

Cat lovers will agree that each cat has a story of their own and some kitties just appear to us in some fashion or another and worm their way right into our home and into our hearts before we even know what is happening. We once had as many as nine cats, and today we are down to just three felines sharing our home. With Baybé gone we are down to just three boys.

The same nephew Gabe, who brought Molly to us years ago, found three kittens living in a hole in the bottom of a tree. Mary raised all three, and we kept a little champagne-colored kitty we named Crockett. He has been with us for fifteen years now and one cool thing about him is that since he was a kitten, he has slept in our bed beside Mary every single night.

I received a call one day from William Lee Golden, who had just adopted a kitten for his son Solomon not realizing that Sol was incredibly allergic to cats. So I went and picked up the kitty and brought him home to Mary. Golden had named him Buttercup, but we renamed him Mitty, as in Mitty the Kitty. He has grown into being one big orange-and-white cat and we really love him. He is around twelve years old now, and when Mary has to yell at him for getting into something, she will call him Buttercup!

Our latest addition, Barney, is quite the story as well. I saw him the first time in a local pet shop several years ago and tweeted out that if I have learned anything at all about cats this guy is special and really needs a good home. Well, a good friend came and adopted him and had him for a few years and then passed away.

Poor Barney was in the house with a dead owner for three days before our Sumner County Sheriff found them and took Barney to a shelter. Mary and I went and picked him up and brought him home, and I was right to begin with. Barney IS a great cat, and he has become a very special friend to me personally during the days of the pandemic and well beyond. He has a little post-traumatic stress syndrome from his awful experience, but we have brought him through as best as we have been able, and we love him very much.

So, yes, cats have become a huge part of our lives, and we have dearly loved them all. If I may paraphrase Mr. Clemens once again, "A home without a cat may be a perfect home . . . but how can it prove its worth?"

Cats are like little pieces of artwork that may puke on your manuscript, but I can't imagine life without them. Most of our kitties have moved on to that better place God has prepared just for them, and I believe in my heart of hearts that one day we will see each cat again. Call me crazy, but that's what I believe.

There was once a tough little feral, who we named Little Tyke, that came around every day for a handout. We were never able to get close to L.T., but we tried to let him know he was loved. One day he didn't show up and it made us so very sad. Stephen King once wrote that outside kitties rarely get to "grow old by the fire" and that has proved to be oh so true. We never knew what happened to the little guy, but we put up a memory stone with his name on it in our kitty cemetery.

Update: On July 4, 2023, our Sabrina called from work and told us someone dumped a kitten in the Havertys furniture store parking lot. Well, we went and picked up this little black-and-white kitten and named her Maggie Mae. Mary had said no to another cat, but this one spoke to our hearts, and now little Maggie rules our home!

However, as fate would have it as this book goes to press, a new kitten has showed up at our farm. We're not sure how he got there but we took him in and named him Jack so now we have five cats and I'll tell you, sometimes having five cats seems like having no cats and other times it's like the Hemingway House in Key West . . . MEOW!

As this book is being finished, our home is shared with five kitties: Crockett, Mitty, Barney, our now reigning princess, Maggie Mae, and Jack.

CHAPTER 45

"HEY, THAT'S US SINGING WITH PAUL SIMON!"

I see myself in New York at the famed A&R Studios recording the song "Slip Slidin' Away" with Paul Simon and legendary producer Phil Ramone. We met Paul at the Grammy Awards and asked him if he would write a song for us as we were passing away quickly on Columbia Records at the time.

Paul told us he was selfish with his songs and, if he wrote a good one for us, he would no doubt end up recording it himself, and that is kind of what happened. However, he did fly us to New York so we could record it with him.

I see myself observing pure genius in the studio, and all that work was certainly worthwhile as "Slip Slidin' Away" became a monster, worldwide hit, which earned for us a Paul Simon *Greatest Hits, Etc.* gold album (although we didn't have a thing to do with Julio down by the schoolyard).

I see myself years later at a fancy hotel in New York City as the Oaks received the prestigious American Eagle award for musical excellence on the same night Billy Joel was honored, and producer Phil Ramone was with him. We had a great time reminiscing about those days in the studio with Paul, eating great food, pitching baseball cards (the New York way), and sitting in a circle finding our harmony parts, while Paul strummed on a huge-sounding Martin 12-string guitar.

I see myself stopped at a red light in Hendersonville, Tennessee, hearing "Slip Slidin' Away" blaring out of a car radio and rolling down my window and yelling, "HEY, THAT'S US SINGING WITH PAUL SIMON!"

Most people didn't realize it was us at the time, but we knew it, and "Slip Slidin' Away" became a life-altering experience for the Oak Ridge Boys.

CHAPTER 46

We were singing and that was all that mattered.

I see myself singing with the Keystones in Upstate New York in a Primitive Baptist church that was not near as long as our old General Motors 4104 bus parked beside it. I see us carrying in our speakers and amps and fitting them gingerly on the small stage beside the pulpit.

The bathroom was in the tiny foyer and, again, the church was so small that as we sang you could hear the bathroom toilet flush. I can see myself trying hard not to laugh out loud as we sang "In the Garden" to the thirty or so people who were sitting in the pews.

Like so many small churches, they would take up a special love offering for the singers—more times than not, there appeared to be a lot more love than offering in the plate. But hey, we were singing and that was all that mattered. 🎤

CHAPTER 47

"Joe, I really don't want to be dealing with all of this . . . I just want to sing!"—Glen Payne

I see myself on a rainy Friday night after getting off work an hour earlier than usual driving all the way to Lancaster, Pennsylvania, in the rain to a Cathedrals Quartet performance at McCaskey High School and getting there just in time to buy a ticket and take my seat as they began to sing. Not only were they (along with the Couriers) my favorite gospel group, but Glen Payne and George Younce were to become mentors and friends for most of my life until God called each one home.

Now if you are a fan of gospel music and Bill Gaither Homecoming videos, I don't have to tell you how amazing these men were and, if you are not, just look them up. Glen was one of the finest singers in history, and I have often said that along with our own Duane Allen, Randy Owen of Alabama, and Ronnie Dunn, Glen Payne was among the best pure vocalists in my lifetime. And George was the best bass singer to ever take the stage.

My Keystone group would often tour with the Cathedrals, and I would always ride on THEIR bus to glean from their experience and knowledge of pure singing. I could write a chapter on these men, and I have actually done that in my book *On the Road with The Oak Ridge Boys*. But right now, seeing myself riding and singing songs with these men is one of my fondest memories.

I see myself visiting with Glen Payne a week before he died of liver failure and him saying to me, "Joe, I really don't want to be dealing with all of this . . . I just want to sing!"

I just want to sing! That moment between us is seared into my heart and always will be. There has also been nothing more memorable than coming home from a trip and Mary telling me there were messages on my phone from George. I see myself rolling with laughter at the corny jokes and crying tears when he would tell me how much he loved me.

I miss these men who stood upon a crossroad and taught me so much about Jesus, life, and pure singing. They were the best!

CHAPTER 48

1998 was quite the year for me.

I see myself in 1998! What a year this was in my life as I
turned fifty years old, and a plethora of memorable events
took place. I lost a good friend in our legendary bus driver
Harley Pinkerman to cancer. My daughter Jennifer married Dan
Stevens. My grandson Luke was born. My sister, Nancy, and I
moved my parents from their long-time home on Jasper Street
to the Southeastern Veterans Center—or as my mom called it,
the "Soldiers Home"—where she wanted to be after two diabetic comas proved she could no longer provide for Daddy the
constant care he needed. And besides, the old neighborhood
where I grew up was turning to crap as gangs and drugs and
prostitution were becoming commonplace. Even though I had
a terrific security system installed, Mommy didn't feel safe there
anymore, and who could blame her.

She had everything worked out with the Veterans Association long before that fall day in 1998, but it was still sad following the ambulance that carried them both from the home
where she worked so hard to Spring City, Pennsylvania, and the
Soldiers Home where they would live until 2001, when Jesus
called them both home.

In 1998 Mary and I purchased a 350-acre farm on the Ten-
nessee/Kentucky state line, which has become my fortress of

solitude over all these years. Mary and I once dreamed of having a second home on an island somewhere, but that little dream faded as years went by. We would never have the time or the finances to keep up with a faraway island home.

Well, one day an old gospel singing buddy told me about a 50-acre tract of land for sale on a mountaintop in Tennessee down near the Alabama state line, so we drove south to see it. We sat up on that quiet mountain for several hours enjoying God's beauty and decided we didn't want to buy this place. However, a nice piece of land somewhere not too terribly far from our home on Old Hickory Lake in Hendersonville could be cool if we could find the right property.

For a couple years I would come home from a road trip, and Mary and I would drive out into the country following every lead regarding land for sale. And then one day we heard about a farm on the TN/KY state line. Lots of rolling hills and pastures and woods, with a log cabin and a guest cabin, two barns, and two and a half miles of creek running through it all. It was once a horse farm and the horse whisperer and his family who owned the place were very motivated to sell as he was wanting to move up to Louisville as soon as he could.

I see myself as we first drove down into that holler and just knew we had to have this place, where the nearest human being lived three miles away. I had made good in the stock market in those days, and selling Pepsi and Intel stock would pay for half. We owned a forty-foot Chris-Craft Express Cruiser that we would sell and put that money into tractors, cutters, chainsaws, weed eaters, John Deere Gators, and such that I still have today. We would finance the rest and try to pay it all off as quick as possible over the coming years, and we have done just that.

As of this writing (2023) we have owned our farm for twenty-five years, and it has become a place for hard work and refuge from a crazy world for our entire family. Our daughters adore this land that God has given us to tend, and our grandchildren have grown up here, and now seeing our little great-grandson, Chance, enjoying the farm has been a tremendous blessing.

Our farm is just an hour-and-twenty-minute drive from Hendersonville, so I find myself here quite often mowing grass or trimming weeds or running my big John Deere 5410 pulling a ten-foot rotary cutter around one pasture or another a long way from Jasper Street in Philly. Sometimes I just sit on the front porch late at night and watch the moon rise above the tree line. It's so quiet here. I think of Jasper Street, where there was NEVER a quiet night. No, not one. There were always cars going by or the distant sounds of trains or people arguing and fighting and cursing, and bottles breaking. But not here.

Yes, I bought a farm in 1998, and it may be the greatest thing I have ever done. As a side note, the Tennessee Titans also moved to Nashville from Houston in 1998, and I bought two seats that my family has enjoyed for decades, especially my grandson, Luke.

He and I have gone to Titans games since he was a little boy. He will always remember going to games with his Pop-Pop much like I remember going to games with my father.

"We are making memories, Pop-Pop," he would always say. Yeah . . . 1998 was quite the year for me. 🎤

CHAPTER 49

I am a better man, and I believe the Oak Ridge Boys are better men today, because of all the quality time spent with Kenny over several decades.

I see myself with Kenny Rogers!

I loved Kenny long before he became the Gambler and one of the biggest stars in the world. And long before the Oak Ridge Boys and the Sweet Music Man were joined at the hip.

As a young man I thought the First Edition was one of the coolest groups ever. While living in Buffalo, their *Rollin' on the River* television show was beamed into my apartment every week. Kenny's raspy voice featured on such songs as "Just Dropped In (To See What Condition My Condition Was In)" and the Mel Tillis–penned "Ruby, Don't Take Your Love to Town" and Kenny's own "The King of Oak Street," and so many more just blew my mind.

I once drove to Toronto to see them in person, and I left with even more love and respect for Kenny and the First. I near cried when they broke up and Kenny moved to Nashville—but what a move that turned out to be.

In 1978, our manager, Jim Halsey, and Kenny's manager, Ken Kragen, got together and planned out the first arena tour in the history of country music. Kenny was now riding the wave

of "The Gambler" and "Lucille," and he and Dottie West were
having huge success as a duet. And we were the hottest young
group in the business, winning awards and having lots of country airplay under our belts, so the "Full House Tour" was born.
We played ninety cities with Dottie and Kenny—and we
never saw an empty seat. A huge, big-time stage was built in
the middle of the arena each night, and Dottie would open the
show and later join Kenny on a few hits like "Every Time Two
Fools Collide."

Then we hit the stage and tore it up every show. To this
day so many fans say they first saw us with Kenny on the "Full
House Tour." After intermission each night Kenny Rogers came
out and proved he was indeed the biggest star in all of country
or pop music, and the friendship and knowledge gleaned from
K.R. meant the world to us.

After that tour, "Elvira" and "Bobbie Sue" hit big for us, and
we were able to take all we had learned from Kenny and hit the
road on our own big arena tour that became the stuff of legend.
The Oak Ridge Boys "Cookin' Tour" featured a never-seen-
before production and, again, we never saw an empty seat well
into 1983.

Then in 1984 and 1985, while we were singing "American
Made," "It Never Hurts to Hurt Sometime," and "Ozark Moun-
tain Jubilee," Kenny invited us to accompany him and Dottie,
and sometimes Dolly Parton, on a "Reunion Tour." By then
Kenny had recorded "Lady," and many other big hits, including
"Islands in the Stream" with Dolly, so again away we went.

Thanks to "Elvira," "Bobbie Sue," and Kenny Rogers, we
had quite a run there of seven straight years playing to sold-out
arenas, averaging around 18,000 people a night. Then Kenny
invited us to go on a Christmas tour with him and an up-and-
comer named Garth Brooks, and we realized we could do our

own Christmas tour. Thanks to Kenny, we have taken to the road for well over thirty years on a monster Christmas tour of our own every November and December.

As years passed, we joined Kenny on one event after another, and when we were inducted into the Country Music Hall of Fame we asked if Kenny could be the one to induct us—and he did.

How much did Kenny Rogers mean to me? His friendship meant the world. I am a better man, and I believe the Oak Ridge Boys are better men today, because of all the quality time spent with Kenny over several decades. One morning in March of 2020 I was just waking up when my Mary yelled to me that Kenny Rogers had died. It was surreal he was gone. A million memories flooded through my heart and mind. Memories of the Sweet Music Man from the First Edition days to becoming a bigger-than-life superstar as well as a mentor and a brother. And even though we shared so much time together over the years, I never stopped being a fan. 🎤

CHAPTER 50

"I will throw you a star!"

I see myself with Nana Gertrude Clark. When I was little, Daddy worked one factory job after another and Mommy worked two jobs at a time to make ends meet. So we put our upstairs back bedroom up for rent and, before Nana showed up, there were a plethora of unique folks who would rent out that room.

We once had a young couple from the former Czechoslovakia living with us for about six months. They had escaped from behind the Iron Curtain on a bicycle. They even had a newspaper article to prove the fact. Little Joey thought that was cool even though he had no idea what the Iron Curtain meant. It was hard for a little boy to process a huge curtain made of iron, but there are so many things adults say that go by unexplained to tiny ears, leaving a child only to imagine and wonder what any of it means.

For example, when I was four years old, I had my tonsils taken out and right before a woozy little boy was wheeled to the "operating room"—which was frightening enough—I heard the doctor say to my mother that while he was "in there" he would be "removing my adenoids as well"!

What? My ADENOIDS? I had no idea what my adenoids were and, to be honest, I still don't. But I digress.

Next up in the back bedroom was an older German lady named Emma Stanke. She was nice enough but her and Daddy fought World War II repeatedly at dinner. Over time, the "crazy old Nazi" just left without a word, and I can't say I blame her. Old Emma had left Germany when she was just a little girl and was nowhere near the Hedgerow battles in France. But Daddy had a lot of scars and lost a lot of friends on those battlefields, and poor Emma got an earful every day.

But then, God sent an angel to our doorstep. We called her Nana right away and for her room and board she would happily look after and help raise little Joey while Mommy and Daddy worked. Along with my mom, Nana Gertrude Clark would become the single biggest influence on my boyhood years.

I was with her most of the time, and she was just the sweetest soul. She grew to really love me, and I loved her back with every fiber of my being. Nana and I would walk across Harrowgate Square on many an afternoon and stroll down Kensington Avenue.

Kensington ran right under the elevated train, and it was a shopping mecca for the surrounding neighborhoods. Five-and-dime stores, banks, supermarkets, shoe stores, meat markets, poultry stores complete with live chickens they would kill right in front of you and then chop them up, movie theaters, restaurants, and even a soft pretzel factory where we always stopped for fresh, hot pretzels right out of the oven.

I can't eat a Philly soft pretzel today without thinking of Nana Clark. Right past the Allegheny Avenue El Station was a hobby shop and a bookstore, and I couldn't wait to get there. I always had a few bucks saved up and burning a hole in my pocket, so I would buy a model plane or ship, or my favorite . . . model birds. And if I had any extra cash, I might pick up some glue or some paints. I have never been very artistic. In fact,

I still draw stick figures for people and little v's for birds in flight. So, to be honest, my models were never very well put together. However, I did enjoy the process.

Then there was . . . the book store! Books new and used for sale here. Nana taught me to love books, for which I will always be grateful. Zane Grey, H. G. Wells, Jack London, and Jules Verne, along with a heavy dose of the classics and God's Holy Word all shaped the imagination of a little Philadelphia kid. I never lost interest in reading, learning, and expanding my knowledge of the make-believe as well as the real worlds existing far from our tiny little two-story rowhouse on Jasper Street.

Nana Clark eventually moved away to a small apartment in West Philadelphia after my sister, Nancy, got big enough to need a room of her own. Nancy got the middle bedroom upstairs that we both shared for many years, and I was awarded the back room.

Mommy and Daddy slept in the front room. Except for a few closets, a hallway, and a small bathroom—that was it for upstairs. I think I was around twelve years old when Nana Clark left, but I still went to visit her almost every weekend. I would happily give up hanging with friends or playing baseball to go see Nana for a day.

It took two city buses and a subway ride to get to Upland Street in West Philly, and there in the middle of the block in the same kind of row house lived Nana. Her first floor rented area had a nice bedroom, a kitchenette, and a very small bathroom. Under her bed she would keep an army cot and a quilt for Joey. I would lie in my army cot at night right next to her bed and listen to her tell stories until we would both fall asleep.

I shared every moment of my life with her as well, and she was always interested and focused, and her input was always memorable and useful. We would then pray together and

I would try so hard to get to sleep first because the old woman, even though she was getting frailer by the month from fighting cancer, could STILL snore like a jackhammer!

Like my mom, she always encouraged me to always be my very best and to put God first in my life. Nana died as I turned fourteen. I visited her in her room at the Philadelphia General Hospital and spent several hours with her before she left us.

A very small and thin Nana Clark told me things that day I have never forgotten. "Don't be so hard on your daddy, Joey. The drinking and his rage at times are all because of that war. Not that this is an excuse, but it IS a reason. Your dad loves you, Joey, and he needs you more than ever. Your mother is the most special woman I have ever known. Lillie's heart is full of pure love, and you must always look after her and your sister as well. You, my sweet boy, are so very special. You worry about things too much and that is why that asthma of yours kicks up like it does. You need not worry about anything, Joey, because you are going to live a long and wonderful life. You know why? Because I will always be looking after you."

So amazing that in less than a year after Nana left this earth my daddy would suffer his stroke and be disabled for the rest of his life. He WOULD need me more than ever, and I grew to love him more and more as the years passed. They buried my little thin Nana Clark in a blue-flowered dress, and within days of her funeral I had a massive asthma attack. I had fought bronchial asthma since I was born, and I was certain I might pass away.

They rushed me to the hospital in an ambulance. Later that night after Mommy and Daddy went home, I lay in my bed all alone, wheezing and coughing. Then a bright light appeared at the foot of my bed. The light moved off to the side just a bit and there stood Nana Gertrude Clark still dressed in her blue-flowered dress smiling at me.

She looked healthy and all shiny. She whispered to me in a very audible voice, "I told you that you would be all right. I will always love you, and I will throw you a star!"

Then, just like that, she was gone. The nurse said it was probably a night watchman's flashlight that I saw, but I knew better. She was there. Nana Gertrude Clark made a stop on her way to Glory to visit Joey, and I assure you she has INDEED thrown many a star my way over all these years.

As a side note, after that night I NEVER had another asthma attack ever again!

CHAPTER 51

The Oak Ridge Boys sang "Amazing Grace" like never before . . .
One last time for our friend!

I see myself singing "Amazing Grace" for the 41st President
of the United States, George Herbert Walker Bush. Now,
again, this is in no way a political thought but more of a
memory of a respected friendship that actually began in 1983
when as vice president (and later president) Bush announced to
the world the Oak Ridge Boys were his favorite music group.
Our friendship has been well chronicled over all these years, but
what folks may not know was his heartfelt affinity for what may
be considered the greatest hymn of all time.

We sang it for him whenever he would ask. We sang the
song in his living room in Kennebunkport, Maine, and on his
back deck overlooking the North Atlantic, for gathered friends
and neighbors, at the Lobster Pot restaurant, and at the histori-
cal Episcopal church by the sea where he and Barbara attended
often.

We sang it at his home in Houston and even sang it to him
over the phone once while he was in the hospital. We sang it
on the White House lawn, the East Room (with his Cabinet in
attendance), the Oval Office, and aboard Air Force One, as well
as during several command performances at various birthday

celebrations—and, yes, the entire world saw us sing "Amazing Grace" at his funeral.

He asked many times for us to sing at his funeral, and we always promised him we would. But man, did we have to pull off the near impossible to work that out!

The 2018 edition of our annual Christmas tour was scheduled to head out west which meant four straight weeks of being on the road. We heard from Bush's staff that his health was failing, so we were told to pack our funeral suits on the trip west. No matter how this might shake out, we were determined to keep our promise to our friend.

The 41st President was honored with a state funeral in Washington, D.C., on December 5 and would be flown to Houston for another funeral on the morning of December 6 at 10 a.m. at the beautiful Saint Martin's Episcopal Church. This is the same church where we attended the funeral of Barbara Bush in April of 2018.

But now for the logistics. We had a show in Spokane, Washington, on December 5 and a show in Kennewick, Washington, on December 6. The only way we could do this was to find a private jet, and it would have to be a fast one. Our long-time friend and entrepreneur Bruce White came through for us.

We knew Bruce well. He not only owned resort hotels all around the world, but he also owned the legendary Star Plaza Theater in Merrillville, Indiana, where we played for decades. Bruce had his big jet waiting for us in Spokane, and as soon as we got off stage, we grabbed our suits and flew to Houston arriving around 4:30 a.m.

After a quick breakfast and a shower, we arrived at the church and, along with Reba McEntire—who also sang that morning—we met with family and dignitaries and proceeded to a holding area by the choir. When introduced, the four of us stood side by side and gazed down at the flag-draped coffin containing the remains of a president of the United States and a treasured friend.

I said, "We are here, sir, as we promised we would be."

Knowing how tired and nervous we were, I attempted a bit of humor. "You know he always considered himself to be somewhat of a bass singer . . . He was NOT."

Thankfully that got a laugh from those assembled. I then blew an A-flat on the pitch pipe and the Oak Ridge Boys sang "Amazing Grace" like never before . . . One last time for our friend! We rolled back to the airport and flew back to Kennewick, Washington, where we did a Christmas show with about an hour to spare.

As a side note, we have lost our friend Bruce White to cancer since that event. We sang "Amazing Grace" at his funeral as well.

CHAPTER 52

When you take the stage at the Opry you stand within that magic circle.

I see myself singing on the stage of the Grand Ole Opry many times over the years, from the legendary stage of the Mother Church of Country Music's famed Ryman Auditorium to the beautiful Opry House off Briley Parkway in Nashville. Any time the Oak Ridge Boys have been invited to sing at the Opry we have jumped at the chance.

But one night everything changed forever when, in the middle of our show, the late Little Jimmy Dickens walked out on stage dressed like our William Lee Golden—complete with sunglasses, cowboy hat, and a hilarious fake beard! We had no earthly idea what was going on as the audience laughed and applauded the well-loved legendary entertainer.

Well, Jimmy grabbed the microphone and shocked the audience and all of us by saying, "I have always wanted to be an Oak Ridge Boy and tonight I invite them to be a member of our great family here. Boys, you are invited to become members of the Grand Ole Opry. Welcome to the family!"

It was an amazing and humbling experience to be sure. We sang "Elvira" with tears in our eyes after Jimmy left the stage and, when we left the stage, we were greeted by a huge press contingent wanting to get our reactions to what just happened.

I am a man of words, but on this occasion, I had none. It was all too emotional. Jimmy Dickens is long gone now, but backstage at the Opry House a framed photo of the Oaks and Jimmy in his fake beard on that wonderful evening is on full display in a hallway where daily backstage tourist groups can walk by and see it.

I have been asked many times what it feels like to now be a member of the Opry. My answer is that every time we played the Opry it was always an honor, but it was like we were guests. Now that we are members, it's like we are *family*—like a house guest being asked to unpack your things because you are invited to live with us.

I still have no words to really describe it. There is a circle of wood in the middle of the Opry stage that dates way back to the early days of the Ryman. When you take the stage at the Opry you stand within that magic circle.

"The Circle," as it is known, has become as famous as the Opry itself—every Opry star in history has stood upon this very wood and performed live. Hank Williams, Roy Acuff, Hank Snow, Minnie Pearl, Johnny Cash, Elvis Presley, Joe Bonsall . . . Joe Bonsall??

Yes, it is true, along with my Oak Ridge Boy brothers, Duane Allen, William Lee Golden, and Richard Sterban, this street kid from Philadelphia is now an Opry star and part of the greatest family in music history.

I wish my mom were alive to see it.

CHAPTER 53

"You are better than this, Bonsall . . . smarten up!"

I see myself as a troubled teenager hanging out with some older guys in the neighborhood from time to time. These were a bunch of guys who were not one bit like my Blackhawks. Not that we Blackhawk boys couldn't be a bit mischievous from time to time. In fact, one time I threw a rock through Mrs. Hands's window just because she was always so mean to us kids.

Old lady Hands was the kind of person who kept your baseball if it went into her yard. It was a constant war with her. We would sit on her front steps sometimes just to hear her cuss at us.

We had horse and wagons pulling vegetable and fruit wagons up and down the street in those days. My mom called them hucksters. Farmers from out in Lancaster County, Pennsylvania, or Cherry Hill, New Jersey, would lead their horse-drawn wagons down the street and yell out at the top of their lungs, "STRAWBERRIES STRAWBERRIES!" or "GET YOUR FRESH HOMEGROWN TOMATOES WHILE THEY LAST," and all the neighborhood ladies would come out of their homes and line up to buy their wares.

Well, one day we shoveled a bunch of horse manure off the street and put it in paper bags. We placed the bags on Mrs. Hands's doorstep, set them on fire, and rang the doorbell. We would then run like mad and hide just a few feet down an alley way where we could watch her come to the door and stomp out the blaze while stepping ankle deep in horse poop. You can't make that stuff up.

But the time I tossed a rock at her window, a neighborhood beat cop saw me. I ran like all get-out, but he caught up to me in no time. He cuffed me and waited on a paddy wagon to get there. He threw me in the back of that stinking wagon and drove me around for hours. I was so scared. Scared of my father finding out and scared of disappointing my mother. I was so happy when he opened the back double doors and let me out of there.

He took off the handcuffs and said, "Joey, my boy, here is what you are going to do. You are going to pay for that window first off and apologize to Mrs. Hands, and if I ever catch you doing anything like that ever again, I am locking you up. If you liked the wagon, you are going to love jail!"

"Yes sir, thank you sir," I squeaked through my tears as he and another cop got back in the front seat of the paddy wagon and drove off leaving me standing there in the street.

I was so happy I wasn't going to prison, but I still hadn't completely learned my lesson. The older guys that hung out just past Venango Street were quite a step up from rock throwing, and I thought they were the coolest. There were guys named Nooks and Chew and Joey the V—and, by God, they liked me. In fact, Joey the V—whose actual name was Joey Vidra—saved my bacon once over by the garages on Atlantic Street. Dago Frankie and his gang of turds were from the next neighborhood over called Fishtown. Once in a great while they came up to Kensington looking for trouble, and they usually found some.

Now I know calling a guy Dago Frankie is not politically correct in this modern age, but that politically correct stuff didn't exist back then. Frankie called *himself* Dago, for crying out loud!

I had my own little personal laws of the street, but sometimes a good scrap was still hard to avoid.

Law #1. If you walk by a certain corner and get beat up or hassled by thugs, then simply stop going by that corner. I walked the long way around the block to Jones Junior High School many times adhering to that one.

Law #2. If the guy is smaller than you, go ahead and fight him and let the chips fall. If the guy is bigger, run like all get-out. I was thin and fast and very light on my feet, and on more than one occasion my speed kept me away from a confrontation.

Law #3. If a fight is imminent and getting hurt is unavoidable, just do your best.

One day as I was walking by the Jasper Street garages, I came face-to-face with Frankie and the turds. Frankie approached me.

"I don't want any trouble with you, Frank," I said rather weakly as hairs on the back of my neck started to tingle.

Then, much to my surprise Dago Frank extended a hand of friendship. It threw me off guard to the point that I didn't realize it was his left hand he extended. My dumb ass reached out and shook his hand, and he immediately yanked me forward while at the same time bringing up his right fist and landing it squarely on the side of my head.

I was dazed and hurting, but I still charged him and knocked him backwards into a wall. But Frankie, although small in stature, was strong and quick as a cat. He shoved me back and pulled out a knife.

My emotions and adrenaline shifted into high gear, and I'll admit I was scared out of my wits when I saw the knife. Then a miracle took place—Joey Vidra's black '52 Ford coupe drove right up on to the sidewalk and screeched to a halt in front of us. Within seconds Joey the V was out of the car and pounding on Dago Frankie.

Now Joey Vidra was a real character. He was around twenty-two years old and was pretty much the "big guy" in Kensington. Nobody messed with Joey the V. He looked the part, too, with his greasy pompadour hair, white T-shirt, a pack of Camels rolled up in the sleeve, a cig hanging out of one corner of his mouth, tight jeans, and black work boots. Everyone knew that Joey Vidra was connected to the mob on some lower level, so nobody ever messed with him.

It was believed that Joey V ran with the storied K&A gang—K&A standing for the intersection of Kensington and Allegheny Avenues just six blocks from the rowhouses on Jasper Street. Everyone also knew the K&A boys were just a few steps away from the Angelo Bruno crime family, which pretty much had control over perhaps the entire Delaware Valley.

On this day Joey the V was my hero. He waved Frankie's knife in his now bloody face and said, "All right, you Dago bastards, get your asses back to Fishtown, all of you. And I swear if I ever see you around here again you are all dead, and I mean DEAD! Now go home to your mothers."

Vidra was also as Italian as a plate of lasagna, so it was kind of funny hearing him call Frankie a Dago. I never saw Dago Frankie or the turds after that, and Joey invited me to come hang out on his corner. I really thought I was tough stuff hanging out with these guys from time to time until the night Joey the V pulled up to the corner and yelled, "Let's go! There're some guys up in Juniata that need a lesson, and we are the ones that will be teaching!"

So I jumped in Vidra's car with about five other boys and off we went to Juniata, which was a neighborhood just north of us. We pulled up at the Scanlon playground where I had played a little baseball with the Kensington Ramblers, and there were a bunch of tough guys there waiting for us.

Joey and Nooks piled out of the front seat first, and as I pushed the driver's seat forward and began to exit the car some kid kicked me right in the face. While laying back on the Ford's smelly floor bleeding and trying not to cry, another miracle happened. I could hear my mother's voice, my Nana Clark's voice, and perhaps even the voice of Jesus whispering to my soul:

"You are better than this, Bonsall . . . This is not your pathway . . . Get away from these guys now . . . smarten up!"

Yes, I had learned my lesson. I was walking down a dead-end street. It is no wonder that some Christian kids were easily able to talk me into going to a gospel quartet concert and later to an old-fashioned campground in Medford, New Jersey, where Jesus Christ would change my life completely.

I went to the corner one day many weeks later and told Joey Vidra that Jesus had changed my life and I wouldn't be back there anymore. To my great surprise the mighty Joey the V teared up a little, hugged me, and wished me well. I never saw him again! 🎤

CHAPTER 54

One day we will be gone, but our images will still hang in the Rotunda of the Country Music Hall of Fame.

I see myself in the Country Music Hall of Fame!

It has been several years now since we came off the stage of the Grand Ole Opry and our manager/godfather Jim Halsey was there to meet us. He indicated we should not just run home but wait a minute because the president of the Country Music Association wanted a few words with us.

So we all walked into a dressing room and there stood Sarah Trahern, the Chief Executive Officer of the CMA, and her husband. As we entered the room she said, "First off, you guys were great tonight on the Opry, and I just wanted to tell you how excited we all are that you will be joining us onstage this year for CMA Fest downtown. We are honored to have you."

We all kind of answered at once. "Well thank you, ma'am, we are stoked about performing at CMA Fest, and we appreciate the CMA for having us."

Then Sarah dropped the other shoe. "Oh, and I wanted to tell you that you will be the newest members inducted into the Country Music Hall of Fame."

You could have heard a fly walking on the wall wearing sneakers. Our jaws dropped, our eyes misted, and our godfather grinned that knowing smile of his.

WOW . . . the greatest honor of all had just been dropped on us, and we were flabbergasted. Then Mrs. Trahern told us the news would break at a press conference at the Hall of Fame in June and the Medallion Ceremony and the unveiling of our plaque would happen in November.

Now this was the end of March in the year 2015, and she also told us we were not to tell anyone outside of our family the news and neither could our family say anything until June. Somehow, we managed to keep it all under our hats, although we were wanting to shout it from the rooftops.

When the big press conference came, at last, in June, we found out the other inductees were the late Grady Martin the legendary guitar player, whose son would represent him, and in the veteran category it would be the Browns, and in the modern era, it would be the Oak Ridge Boys.

That summer we were the talk of music circles everywhere, and when the big ceremony came in November, we were still not prepared for the honor coming our way that night. Kenny Rogers was there to induct us and even General Chuck Yeager made his way to Nashville to celebrate with us.

The Hall of Fame Theater was packed as Grady, the Browns, and the Oaks were celebrated. Our plaque was unveiled and our medallions were placed around our necks. One day we will be gone, but our images will still hang in the Rotunda of the Country Music Hall of Fame. I offer as an addendum a piece I wrote called "The Rotunda":

> The hallowed Rotunda at the Country Music Hall of Fame in Nashville, Tennessee, is where the plaques of inducted Hall of Famers are mounted in a huge and beautiful circle. "All are equal inside of this circle" is the mantra, and it is a sight to behold.

The words *WILL THE CIRCLE BE UNBROKEN*
are written above the bronzed plaques, and the circular
ceiling that is bathed in sunlight seems to rise above to
the heavens—which is also symbolic, for many of our
country music heroes whom we have loved have moved
on beyond this earth, and their light does indeed seem
to shine down upon the Rotunda.

It is still mind-boggling to me that the Oak Ridge
Boys will be enshrined here come November. So early
this morning I drove down to the "Hall." Bill Cody
was broadcasting live over WSM AM radio from there,
and I was to be his last guest. I was scheduled to appear
around 9 a.m. to talk and laugh with Bill about my new
book *On the Road with The Oak Ridge Boys*, the Oaks'
new hymns CD *Rock of Ages*, the Grand Ole Opry and,
of course, our Hall of Fame induction.

I awakened with the sun and decided to go on
downtown early to beat the Nashville rush-hour traffic
that borders on being horrific on most days. Nashville
is growing by leaps and bounds, which is cool, but
our highway system has not caught up yet. It's like our
politicians are playing Sim City and forgot about traffic
volume, and if I had to do this as many do twice a day,
I would gut myself!

I managed to get to the Hall of Fame almost ninety
minutes before my interview on WSM, and security
guards brought me on up out of the lower-level parking garage on to the main floors, where the exhibits
as well as the Rotunda are on display. It would be an
hour before the Hall opened to the public so, while Bill
Cody interviewed songwriting king Don Schlitz and
songstress Kathy Mattea, I wandered around the Hall

of Fame all alone, and it was one of the greatest experiences of my life.

I have written several editorials and a magazine piece already about the beauty and length and breadth of our new CMHOF and education center, so I won't elaborate. Suffice to say that it is a magnificent tribute to America's country legends of today and yesterday and to the music itself.

There are ghosts everywhere. I talked to John and June this morning. I chatted with George Jones and Tammy Wynette and Conway Twitty. I stood before Earl Scruggs and John Hartford's actual banjos and thanked them for being banjo heroes to Ban-Joey.

I spent some time with Miss Minnie Pearl and the Tater, Jimmie Dickens, and even thanked Ernest Tubb for the signed picture he gave to Mary's father, Albert Bell. It meant the world to him, and it now hangs on our wall at home. I had never met many of these folks, but I was quite amazed at how many I did know and knew quite well.

After my mystical visits, I entered the Rotunda where our own faces would be immortalized in bronze very soon. I set myself down in the very center of the floor cross-legged and took it all in. It was just me . . . all alone on the floor . . . sitting in the middle of the circle that would forever be unbroken. I wept like a child. I could see myself as little Joey singing in his bedroom in Philadelphia. Gospel songs, country songs, and rock songs traversed across the fields of my mind.

I could see myself driving a Buick pulling a trailer through the Western Pennsylvania hills listening to Merle Haggard for hours. I could see myself getting off the plane in October of 1973 to join the Oak Ridge Boys. I could see our entire career play out in my mind. The songs, the miles, the shows, the ups and downs, and I took comfort in the fact it is all far from over.

I could see younger versions of myself and Duane Allen, William Lee Golden, and Richard Sterban dreaming dreams and reaching for the stars and working hard to make sure we did everything the right way, and now I see us HERE! In the Country Music Hall of Fame . . . The ROTUNDA! The greatest honor in a career of honors is to be up on that wall in this circle.

I got up, said a prayer of thanks to my Lord and Savior, and wiped the tears. I had an interview to do and by now Bill Cody and WSM were waiting for me. However, rest assured, I will NEVER forget these moments . . . EVER!

As a side note, upon our plaque beside each of our names and just under our bronze likeness is our birthdates and just beside each date there is a tiny dash. I am thankful that there is nothing written on the other side of our dash just yet, but someday another date will be engraved there.

In the crazy year of 2020, five Hall of Fame plaques had to engrave a date beside the dash as Kenny Rogers, Charlie Daniels, Jan Howard, Harold Reid of the Statler Brothers, and Charley Pride have all gone home. Yes, one day we too will all go home, but for now we will celebrate the dash!

CHAPTER 55

No one can ever fill Billy Graham's shoes, but together we can all give it a try. And together we can shine the light of Jesus Christ, for in HIM there is NO darkness at all.

I see myself writing a story about Billy Graham for a compilation book published right after his death, and I thought it made sense to share it here:*

The Billy Graham Crusade came to my hometown in 1961 for a month-long revival that started at the Philadelphia Civic Center and ended in Memorial Stadium (later renamed JFK Stadium and then torn down in 1992). Over 700,000 people came out to hear Rev. Graham that month, including more than 70,000 a night at Memorial. I was one of those 70,000 for three straight nights near the end of the crusade.

I was thirteen years old and in my formative decision-making years, trying to decide if I wanted to listen to my mother and the good folks at Calvary Church of the Brethren, or hang out on corners and

---

* https://www.amazon.com/Moments-Billy-Graham-Americas-Preacher/dp/16 04950439/ref=sr_1_1?crid=QR1OTAEJEQI2&dib=eyJ2IjoiMSJ9.nGByAGrCn ip8pf9yGXpaf28A63qO-oSRqzP381q0PB23zvWTUfCCRQQghDoRTqPpaJDu 9GGrAbtVdT-zBclJc1uRHYG5EuZ1sIdT7c6ndNwvhlYvtZgetYOSx9MHNofwt u_r

become a street bum. At that point, the wannabe
hoodlums on the corner had the edge. My mom and I
walked three blocks to the church, where three school
buses had lined up to take anyone who wanted to see
Billy Graham.

I'll admit I was excited. I had seen him on television. And in 1961 if you saw someone in person who
had been on television, and if you were thirteen . . .
Well, that was just huge.

A quick example. The year before, my father had
taken me to a Thrill Show at the very same Memorial
Stadium in South Philly. It was acrobatics, motorcycles,
and cool car tricks, and several television stars showed
up—local stars like Sally Star and Carney C. Carney the
clown. But the big star of the night was James Arness,
a.k.a. U.S. Marshal Matt Dillon from the western show
Gunsmoke. Little Joey freaked out seeing the marshal
decked out in his full cowboy attire, complete with a
holster and two fake (I assumed!) six guns.

So I must admit, seeing Billy Graham live and
in person was also kind of exciting to me, and many
others, because for three straight nights there was a
gigantic crowd at the crusades.

The crowd, the music, and the Reverend himself,
as it turned out, would have a powerful impact on me.
Even though I am in my seventies now, and much of it
is a blur, I remember him preaching directly to the city
itself, a place facing a lot of racial division at the time.

He told us only Jesus and His amazing grace could
heal the divides separating us and only the love manifested on the cross could save us from our sin. He also

talked a lot about the promise of heaven. It was amazing, and I was in total awe of this great man.

I wish I could say I went forward as the choir and the masses sang, "Just as I Am." But I did not. I sat by my precious mother and watched her pray, and my heart was filled with love, and a seed was planted that would eventually lead to my accepting Jesus Christ as my very personal Savior a few years later. A decision leading me away from the street life and into a life of music, where I reside today as a member of the American music group the Oak Ridge Boys.

I had never thought much about Jesus until those nights at Memorial Stadium, but afterward He was all I thought about. I believe that God had a plan for my life. And I also believe He kept me from harm in those years before I became a Christian.

Fast-forward to the White House in 1993. The Oak Ridge Boys and our wives had become friends with President George H. W. Bush (#41), and he had just lost the election to William Clinton, so he would not serve a second term. Early that January, President Bush invited us to sing in the East Room for the entire Cabinet and Congressional members. After we performed, we spent the night in the White House, which was all pretty surreal for a kid from Philly, and it was about to become even MORE surreal.

The next morning the president invited us to a special ceremony in the same room where we performed the night before. He was to present former President Ronald Reagan with the Medal of Freedom. We took our seats among the small audience, which was

gathered, and lo and behold, seated right to the left of
my Mary and me was the Reverend Billy Graham! He
was as kind to us as you would imagine he would be. I
shook his hand and fought back tears as he rose and led
the room in a word of prayer.

I wanted to tell him all about how much he meant
to me and about those nights in Philadelphia and how
much my mother loved him and . . . But I did not. I
just took in the moment and held my wife's hand. We
were so privileged to just be in this room at this time,
and we would never forget it.

Now the great man is at home with our Savior in
the place that has been prepared for men such as he.
My mom left in 2001, and I am quite certain she has
found him by now and bent his ear pretty good. The
message of Billy Graham in Philadelphia in 1961 is the
same message needed today. There is much division in
our world, and only Jesus Christ can provide the answer
and the love needed to save us all. We must learn to
stand upon the promises Billy Graham preached about
many years ago.

Where would the world be without the souls who
were saved because of his ministry? Where would I be?

We have a song in country music called "Who's
Gonna Fill Their Shoes." No one can ever fill Billy Graham's shoes, but together we can all give it a try. And
together we can shine the light of Jesus Christ, for in
HIM there is NO darkness at all.

CHAPTER 56

Mary and I have always loved the water.

I see myself on the water. Mary and I have always loved the water whether on an island vacation or here at home living on Old Hickory Lake. I see the two of us, swimming, or deep-sea diving, or snorkeling the reefs from Bonaire to the Cayman Islands to the French Polynesian Isles of Tahiti.

I was very fortunate to have made a good enough living singing in our younger days that we were able to do things together that would have been much harder in our older years. Believe me, Mary and I took full advantage of being young and in good condition. We would sometimes take two vacations a year or whenever the Oak Ridge Boys' schedule allowed for it to happen.

"We have nine days off in a row in November . . . let's go to Jamaica!"

We almost drowned off the far-away island of Huahine, Tahiti. We were paddling around in one of those two-people outriggers the locals call divorce canoes, and for good reason. Well, my dumb ass turned us over and before we knew it the undercurrent was taking us out to sea.

We could not swim against it, so we started to holler "HELP!" and, thankfully, an old salt from Chicago who had sailed all the way from the Great Lakes to Tahiti heard us and immediately jumped in his motorized dinghy. He headed our way and yanked us up and out of the water. That was a close call, and I assure you we have never forgotten it.

Had that sailor not heard us, we would have gone all Tom Hanks out into the Pacific and never returned. That night over dinner the "wife glare" was quite evident, and it was well deserved.

I have also loved to go deep sea fishing from time to time. Even though I have been quite successful fishing the waters from Key West to Belize to the Gulf of Mexico and on to the North Maine Coast with President George H. W. Bush, I have always managed to toss my cookies on just about every trip.

Mary and I once caught THREE sailfish in one day off the coast of Key West. We tagged them and returned them to the sea. However, we have a model and a plaque on our wall chronicling the event.

In Belize I once caught a twenty-five-pound tuna that we cooked up in a firepit on the beach that evening—man, that was some good eatin'. Despite my weak stomach, I would head out to sea with a big rod and reel in my hand in a heartbeat. (I never did puke in front of President Bush; however, he did mention I was getting a bit "green around the gills" out there. You can't hide a thing from a former head of the CIA.)

Yes, that has always been Mary and me—island hopping, sunning, fishing, hiking, snorkeling, scuba diving, and dining on great food. However, the real fun on the water happened for us right here at home. In our thirties we bought our first boat. It was a 19-foot Chaparral runabout, and we waterskied up and down the Cumberland River every chance we got. I could even slalom on one ski with the best of them, and Mary was quite adept at pulling me up and expertly handling the boat.

Next up we traded in our Chaparral for a 21-foot Mirada runabout that still lives in our boat dock today. We are getting a bit old for water skiing these days, but my entire family makes good use of the Mirada. Daughters and grandkids could call at any moment on a summer day asking for permission to "take the boat out!"

In our forties we splurged on a brand new 40-foot Chris-Craft Express Cruiser, complete with a nice kitchen, a guest bedroom, and a master suite. Words cannot express (no pun intended) how much fun we had on that boat. Mary and I cruised three or four days at a time up and down the Cumberland River, anchoring down in a cove somewhere or even along the docks in downtown Nashville.

I have vivid memories of driving that boat between the buoys late at night and Mary appearing from down below with a sandwich and a cup of hot tea for the captain. Cruising the river during the day or night with my special first mate sure was a long way from my busy singing life, and I always took time on the water to thank my Lord Jesus for His blessings.

I hated to sell that big boat, but as I approached my fifties it was buying the 350-acre farm that became my new dream spot. A big John Deere 5410 tractor took the place of the Chris-Craft. I miss that boat sometimes, but cutting a big field around midnight on a hot summer night is not unlike cruising the river in my captain's chair. And cranking up that big tractor is also quite a bit like cranking up those two big Volvo Penta engines on the Chris-Craft. Manly sounds . . . *VROOOOMMMM!*

Once we bought that farm, we never took another island vacation. We decided to save that money and pay off the farm. Perhaps one day we may take one more trip to Caneel Bay, St. John, or perhaps Tahiti, or we may even take an Alaskan cruise.

That would be nice as long as we stay away from one of those divorce canoes.

Sometimes my mind goes back to a young Joe riding around the perimeter of the Yucatan Peninsula's Isla Mujeres on a motorcycle with Mary holding tight around my waist, her pretty face pressed sideways against my back as the wind is blowing sea mist in our faces as we cruise along the cliff side. It makes me cry, not because of a youth gone by, but because of how much I love her.

CHAPTER 57

"Your father was a hero, and I will not throw him away like an old shoe."

I see myself walking to Craftex Mills where my mother worked. The factory was just a few blocks from our house and sometimes my sister, Nancy, and I would take her some lunch, especially if it was on a Saturday.

There was an Irish bar or taproom as we called them right up from the factory where they made my mother's favorite Shrimp Basket, so we loved to surprise her with one. The Shamrock also made a mean roast beef on weck sandwich as well. For years I would go there to get a weck for Daddy.

"Joey, here's some money. Run down to the Shamrock and get Daddy a weck sandwich and pick me up a shrimp basket, will ya?!" A fond memory for certain.

Mom's job at Craftex was as a floor lady in charge of a whole floor, and her duties entailed keeping everyone working on those loud-as-heck yarn machines. You couldn't even hear yourself talk in there, and it was always hotter than a July outdoor show in Mississippi.

I would often see Mom grab a broom and hit some guy who was napping and order him back to work. I always felt sad when I saw how hard she worked there. Her other job was as a salesgirl for the H. L. Green department store over on Frankford

Avenue. After Daddy's stroke, Mom would often work all day at Craftex, come home and cook dinner, and then take the Frankford elevated train to H. L. Green, where she would work until 9 p.m., and then take the El back to the Tioga Street station and walk a block back home.

Neighbors helped look after my sister, and I was also working at the animal hospital after school and on Saturdays. While Daddy was still in the Veterans Hospital in Coatesville, Pennsylvania, we would all get in his old station wagon and drive out there to spend Sunday afternoons with him. It would be a while before he realized who we were, where he was, and what even happened to him.

These were hard days for our small family, but we seemed to become a bit stronger and tougher by the day. Nobody was tougher than Lillie Bonsall. No matter how she felt, she pressed onward looking after her children and making ends meet the best she could. So far there has been nothing as challenging in my life as those days in the first couple of years after Daddy's stroke.

After D-Day, the Hedgerows, and getting blown up in Saint-Lô France, my daddy wasn't afraid of anything. Yet during these crazy years, I saw fear in his eyes for the first time.

Death is quite final, but when a person is cut down by a disease or crippled by a brain-damaging event, one's entire life changes. The previous life has been altered to a point of no resemblance of the former self, and it is heartbreaking to see anyone travel that road, especially a family member.

But again, my mother was a rock. Her faith never wavered. She was always smiling and praying and mothering and being a dedicated wife. As I wrote about her in *G.I. Joe and Lillie*, her mantra was always, "Your father was a hero, and I will not throw him away like an old shoe," and she never did.

As I grew older and pursued my musical dreams with her blessings, and as Nancy grew into a beautiful and very busy young lady, she maintained her love and dedication to my father until that January day in 2001 when he passed away, just nine months before Lillie would join him in the sacred ground of Arlington National Cemetery.

Your author has toured most of the world and has achieved success way beyond his dreams, but I have NEVER met anyone like her. No, not one . . .

The old Women's Army Corp WAC was the toughest, the funniest, and the most loving person I have ever met. I will see her again one day on the promised shore as is His promise and I can't wait.

CHAPTER 58

The names of the players change over the years, but that name on the front of the Jersey in bright red script is timeless to me.

I see myself loving baseball. Ah, yes, as the great Hall of Fame baseball author Roger Angell once wrote, "consider the sphere." And I must say that along with my love for music it has been the sphere, the baseball, and the game itself that has been the foremost passion of my life.

I love baseball, and it all began, of course, with my dad taking me to old Shibe Park, also known as Connie Mack Stadium at the corner of 21st and Lehigh in Philadelphia when I was a little boy.

I loved the Phillies with all my heart and to this day I still follow their every move and every player and every game. We had a very small yard when I was a boy, but once my father tore down an old, useless shed behind our little kitchen, the small piece of cement became just big enough to where a small rubber ball and a ton of imagination could play out entire Phillies games. We threw the ball against what was left of the shed wall and also utilized a huge brick wall beside the yard that was actually the side of the Kane family's house, who lived on Clearance Street. Earl Kane was a policeman, and he would often appear on his back steps and threaten to arrest me if that ball was bounced off the side of his house one more time.

I, of course, would announce the entire make-believe games in my best Byrum Saum voice. I loved the Phillies announcer By Saum, and I could imitate him quite well.

"Hello everybody and welcome to Phillies baseball" or *"There's a long high fly ball to deep left center field . . . that ball is GONE! Callison has again gone DEEEEPPPP against Bob Gibson and this place is losing its mind!"* or *"Phillies baseball is brought to you tonight by Ballantine Ale and Beer, Tastykake cakes and pies and the Atlantic Richfield Company. Keep your car on the go . . . with Atlantic!"*

After the Dodgers and Giants moved to the West Coast, I listened to every late-night game on my little transistor radio that Nana Clark bought for me and pretended to be asleep when my mother checked in on me. I could always fool Mommy but not my father.

"Get that thing out of your ear and turn it off, tomorrow is a school day!"

"Okay, Dad," I would answer. But within moments I was back to listening to By Saum coming to you *"LIVE from Dodger Stadium."*

The Phillies were never very good in those days, but a few years after I joined the Oak Ridge Boys they really started cranking. With players like Bob Boone, Larry Bowa, Greg Luzinski, and my favorite player of all time Mike Schmidt. They actually won the National League East pennant in 1976, 1977, and 1978 but were thwarted in '76 by the Cincinnati Big Red Machine and kept from the World Series in '77 and '78 by the Tommy Lasorda–led Los Angeles Dodgers.

As the Oaks began to achieve success, we became friends with many of the Dodgers, Phillies, and even the Houston Astros. Our best friend in those days was Houston knuckleballer Joe Niekro, and in 1980 when the Phillies added Pete Rose to the mix, their pathway to winning their first-ever World Series against the Kansas City Royals ran right through Houston. Joe Niekro made certain Richard and I were in attendance for all three historic playoff games in the Astrodome that year. When the Phillies won that series, we were in the clubhouse with them as they all sang our song, "Dig a Little Deeper in the Well," while shooting champagne all around the clubhouse.

Our friends with the Phillies, which included the big right-handed reliever Ron Reed, made sure Richard and I were seated in Veterans Stadium to witness the World Series, and for that I will always be grateful. The very next year a childhood dream came true. In a three-game home stand against the Astros, the Phillies allowed me to wear a uniform and take batting and fielding practice with the team, and they let me hang out with the players in the clubhouse and dugout.

Catching fly balls in the outfield off the bat of Mike Schmidt, while "Elvira" blared out of the stadium speakers was a highlight of my life! One of my first published pieces was called "Daydreams . . . Joe Bonsall's Greatest Hit," which chronicled the event in *Country Music Magazine*.

Because of the Oak Ridge Boys and our singing of the National Anthem at so many huge baseball events through the years, I have met legends and childhood heroes like Mickey Mantle, Roger Maris, Stan Musial, Ernie Banks, and so many more.

I was never good enough to play professional baseball myself; in fact, in two years of playing little league ball for the Kensington Ramblers, I never even started. My arm was weak, so I had to play second base, and I still squinted a bit when a hard grounder or grasscutter came my way, sometimes going right "through the wickets" because I didn't "get my gate down" enough.

But one of my most memorable moments came in the Phillies clubhouse in 1981 chatting with Pete Rose when I told him how honored I was to be there with the team. Pete asked, "Do you remember the best player you ever saw growing up in little league, high school, college, or even the minors? That kid had a rat-ass chance of EVER making it to the Major Leagues. Well, Joe, how many bands are playing "Elvira" in Holiday Inns and bar rooms tonight while YOU are playing the song to sold-out arenas! You belong here, man . . . you are big league, Joe . . . Yep, you belong here."

I never forgot it! These days I cheer for Harper and Nola and Schwarber and Turner. Yes, the names of the players change over the years, but that name on the front of the jersey in bright red script is timeless to me: PHILLIES! 🎤

CHAPTER 59

VIVA LAS VEGAS!

I see myself in Las Vegas!

Back in 1975, when our godfather stood at the crossroads and changed the very trajectory of the Oak Ridge Boys, one of the first things he did was book us for a three-week stint headlining the Landmark Hotel in a show called "Country Music Tonight," which also featured various comedians and such as opening acts.

We didn't have the proverbial pot, yet here we were performing our mix of gospel and country songs in a Vegas showroom. Howard Hughes pretty much ran Las Vegas in those days, and his show promoter was a man named Walter Kane. Jim Halsey and Kane were close friends and because of that friendship, country music stars like Roy Clark, Mel Tillis, Dottie West, and even up-and-comers like the Oak Ridge Boys ruled the Las Vegas Strip.

Jim was also a man of his word as every single show at the Landmark was chock-full of talent buyers from all over the country. Once they saw us onstage, the date book would begin to fill up with fairs, theaters, and college campus shows, so the philosophy certainly panned out.

After a few stints at the Landmark, we began to open for Roy Clark at another Hughes property, the famous Frontier

Hotel. By the time 1980 rolled around with five gold albums under our belt, we headlined the Frontier by ourselves. And in just a few short months we were headlining the Celebrity Showroom at the new MGM Grand Hotel.

Later when the MGM turned into Bally's, we crossed the street to headline the Circus Maximus Theater at Caesars Palace, which we considered to be rather "high cotton." Previously I had seen the Osmond Brothers and Andy Williams play on that stage, as well as George Burns, Diana Ross, and others, and now the Oak Ridge Boys were singing on that same legendary stage. After about three years at Caesars, we went back across the street to Bally's and that run lasted another several years.

Now we still dip into Las Vegas from time to time, but those days I just wrote about were exciting, magical, and quite unforgettable. I so enjoyed hitting the stage at these various big-time Las Vegas venues. We were treated like kings and much history was made for ourselves, our supporting acts like Lee Greenwood, Exile, the Dirt Band, Patty Loveless, and others. Dare I say, under our godfather's guidance we made history for country music itself.

On a personal note, Mary and I always had a blast in Las Vegas. It was like a vacation for us, even though I usually had to play two shows a night. It is interesting to me that the Landmark and Frontier have since been torn down and the Celebrity Theater at Bally's as well as the legendary Circus Maximus at Caesars Palace are also long gone.

Like everything else, Las Vegas is different than it used to be as huge production events like Cirque du Soleil, Broadway shows, and others now rule the Strip as opposed to a marquee reading, *Walter Kane Presents The Oak Ridge Boys*. But it is still fun to drop in on occasion and play for three days or so at the

Golden Nugget or perhaps the Orleans, eat at Vic & Anthony's, or Battista's Hole in the Wall, a favorite since 1980, where we are still treated like kings! VIVA LAS VEGAS!

CHAPTER 60

Whether I am on the road sitting in the back of the tour bus, or on that blessed front porch . . . you will find Ban-Joey playing "banjer" and enjoying every second.

I see myself playing the banjo.

It all started years ago when on a flight to Seattle I found myself sitting next to the great banjoist Ned Luberecki. After the obligatory banjo jokes, we started to discuss the history of the banjo and why it was important to music past and present. By the time we landed I was convinced that I needed to learn to play the banjo, and the one thing I did not count on was that, like most art forms, the banjo was not easy to learn. Yet I persevered and, after a few years, I was getting there.

Over these years I have grown to love the instrument. I love the drive and the sound and the power that it brings to a bluegrass band or even to a modern country music track. I still consider myself a student of the instrument and probably always will. Even though I work hard at it and practice diligently, my skill set will never allow me to be a top-tier player like a Jimmy Mills or a Sammy Shelor. But that is not really my goal anyway.

No professional banjo players are in any danger from Ban-Joey. In my early days of playing, my main goal was to just make it sound somewhat like a banjo, and this goal I have accomplished. So many great players over the years have helped me out by teaching me new rolls and new licks, adding to my banjo vocabulary, and for this I am very grateful.

The banjo community is a very cool group and very special, and my Ban-Joey character has at least managed to garner a lot of respect from those players of all levels that enjoy the 5-string! Now I realize that many do not share my love for the banjo, so I make sure that when I play, I am well out of earshot of those who may not want to hear it. It is called banjo etiquette.

Mark Twain once said, "A gentleman is one who can play the banjo but does not." (Paraphrased a little, but you get the point.)

Sometimes at home all I need to do is unlock the banjo case and my cats and even my wife run for the hills before I even get the thing out. But that's okay. What is pure heaven to me though is sitting on my front porch at our farm all alone on an early spring evening with my banjo on my knee and a glass of good Cabernet by my side. Nobody lives close to me out there except for coyotes, turkeys, bobcats, and barn swallows, and I don't think they mind a little "Foggy Mountain Breakdown" cutting through the warm air.

As I always say, after all these years of picking I really should be better, but isn't everything we do a constant process with a learning curve attached? I will admit to being a bit of a slow learner, but I do stay at it. My style is mostly Earl Scruggs three-finger bluegrass, however I do enjoy experimenting. It takes me awhile to learn melodic runs, but they sure sound cool when incorporated.

I have done a little studio work from time to time, and I am very thankful for patient producers who have given me a chance to lend a bit of Ban-Joey texture to a rocking track or maybe even let loose a good solo run as I do on the Oak Ridge Boys *Rock of Ages: Hymns and Gospel Favorites* album on "Power in the Blood." And also on "Standing in the Need of Prayer" on our album *Back Home Again.*

Yep—that's me! I have several great-sounding banjos. A man can't have too many banjos, in my humble opinion. Here is my list: a Sonny Osborne Chief, a Deering Tenbrooks, a Deering Electric Crossfire, a Deering Goodtime (Opry edition), a Gibson Granada, two stunning Gretsch models courtesy of my banjo hero and friend Todd Taylor, and my favorite kicking banjo right now is a custom-made Gibson built for me by Todd. Man, it will peel paint off the wall!

My friend and brother Todd Taylor is a legend and a banjo hero. He is in the *Guinness Book of World Records* as the fastest banjo player in history, and he has taken banjo playing to so many new levels over the years from a worldwide perspective. Look him up.

So, while singing and writing are the main cogs in my wheel, playing the banjo has also become a huge part of my life, and I feel that I am better for it. Except for some half-baked piano, I have never played an instrument. Not even a guitar! So being able to pick has been a tremendous accomplishment for me.

Rest assured that on most days, whether I am on the road sitting in the back of the tour bus, or on that blessed front porch, or perhaps inside of a picking circle somewhere, you will find Ban-Joey playing "banjer" and enjoying every second.

PICK!

CHAPTER 61

"The Right Stuff"

I see myself and the Oak Ridge Boys being friends with our nation's greatest aviator, General Chuck Yeager. It all started around thirty years ago in Myrtle Beach, South Carolina, while doing a show at one of our favorite places to play, the Alabama Theater.

We were doing a meet-and-greet with radio station contest winners when a stage manager came back and said, "There's a Chuck Yeager knocking on the stage door, says he just wants to meet the group."

"WHAT? CHUCK YEAGER? Bring him back here."

And within just a few minutes we were shaking hands with "The Right Stuff." He told us he didn't have tickets to the show, but he drove by and saw the bus and just wanted to say hi to his favorite group.

He was in town for a reunion with some of his flight wing buddies from World War II. Well, we secured tickets for Yeager and his fellow pilots and began a friendship that lasted until he passed away in early 2020, just before his ninety-eighth birthday.

The General would attend countless shows around the country over the years. We never knew just when he would show up—and when he did, he always went out on stage before the show and introduced us to the crowd, who would stand and cheer for him. It was always a wonderful moment. We sang at his eightieth birthday celebration—from then on, we shared his birthday every single year up until number ninety-seven. I remember a story a fellow pilot shared with us.

"We were flying in formation on the French Coast about a month after D-Day when Chuck came on the radio saying, 'Three bogies at 3 o'clock . . . Messerschmitt.' Well, we were stymied because none of the other pilots could see a thing but lo and behold within a few moments there they were. Yeager could see them long before the rest of us. Suffice to say, we shot them all down!"

Throughout the years I had the privilege of spending quality time with the General, and I will never forget these conversations with an American hero.

"I flew a P-51 over your daddy on D-Day. Those boys down there were the guys who had it tough. I was always above the fray and providing cover for them. It was hell down there."

How about this:

"I hated getting shot down that one time, but being I survived, it all ended up being a great experience for me. A small town in France took me in for a time when I really needed a break. The girls were pretty, and the wine flowed like water. It was a fun time because for just a few days it seemed like there was no war going on. But there was, and I was happy to get back in the sky and shoot down more enemy. I was really good at it!"

And, of course, there was breaking the sound barrier.

"I was scared, but what the hell—somebody had to do it, and I figured that somebody was me!"

The General was in the audience the night we were inducted into the Country Music Hall of Fame, which was an honor beyond our imagination. Over the years he became somewhat of a father figure to all of us. We all loved General Chuck Yeager, and he loved us.

In later years when he was wheelchair bound, he would sit on the side of the stage and cheer us on especially when we sang his favorite song, "It Takes a Little Rain." Duane Allen would always look over and smile at him as he sang the verses, and the General would raise a fist in the air and his face would just light up.

At show's end, his wife, Victoria, would wheel him out onstage, and we would gather around him and sing "Bobbie Sue," as the crowd would stand and cheer. You just don't forget moments like this.

Rest in peace, General Chuck Yeager. Your friendship meant the world. You were the best of us!

CHAPTER 62

God placed a veterinarian at the crossroads just when I needed him.

I see myself as a veterinarian's assistant. I worked part-time for Dr. Frederick R. Rude at his small animal hospital on Frankford Avenue in Philly, and his guidance was immeasurable during those crazy years in my life. I started as a kennel boy, which basically meant cleaning up dog and cat poop. But eventually because of my interest in animal medicine, I moved up to become a full-fledged veterinary assistant.

I did everything for Dr. Rude. I kept all the patient records, guided the patients and their owners to the right examining rooms, assisted the doctor in every examination, and in most every surgery ran the centrifuge and tested fecal material and was able to ascertain if a dog or kitty had worms and could even tell what kind of worms they had. I looked after and fed hospitalized animals and boarded animals as well and, yes, along with a coworker named Tommy Maddox, still cleaned up a ton of poop.

I was working for Dr. Rude when the call came that my dad had been injured at work and taken to a hospital. They found him slumped over a machine he was fixing at American Steel Engineering Company and thought he might have been electrocuted. The doctor closed the animal clinic and drove me to the hospital.

When I arrived, my mom was already there and eventually the doctors realized that my father had a stroke. It seemed that a piece of shrapnel lodged in his carotid artery, and they feared his brain was permanently damaged.

Those fears would come to be realized over the next several years at one veterans facility after another. But, oh how much Dr. Rude meant to me in those days. He was a man of faith, and he planted a lot of positive seeds of wisdom in my heart I have never forgotten to this day.

These were the formidable days of my life, sandwiched between the streets and becoming a Christian, and I needed his leadership and influence. Becoming a veterinarian was not in the cards for me, but the things I learned in that little animal hospital have never left me. I have come to realize quite often that God placed Dr. Frederick R. Rude at the crossroads just when I needed him.

We managed to stay close over all these years too. Whenever I would go home to visit, I would always stop by to visit him to chat about new advances in pet medicine, how my life was going, and perhaps share a word of prayer. The doctor eventually retired and once, while he and his wife were touring around the country, he stopped by our home in Hendersonville, Tennessee.

It was such an honor to have him here. While touring the living room he was quite enamored by a beautiful urn-like piece on the living room mantel. Mary, without hesitation, said, "Oh, that's my aunt Bessie."

He almost fainted. It was a funny moment.

He also came out to an Oak Ridge Boys show on several occasions and was always so proud of me. He passed away recently. Dr. Rude was such a good man, and a great veterinarian, and I miss him. 🎤

CHAPTER 63

The Alumnus of the Year in 1982 . . . Joseph S. Bonsall.

I see myself in 1982 being honored by my alma mater, Frankford High, with their prestigious Alumnus of the Year award. At a ceremony held in the school auditorium, there were dignitaries and members of the press from all over the city and state, as well as my family, my three Oak Ridge Boys partners, and people like Dr. Rude, Mr. Hamilton, and Jim Halsey, who have all stood at many of the crossroads in my life. The senior class of '82 was also gathered, and I had the opportunity to bring to them as positive a message as I could about working hard and following your dreams and putting God first.

It was an unforgettable day as I never dreamed that the Joey—who once walked through these halls and passed this wall of fame every single day—would one day have my own photo up there. If you were to visit FHS today, you would see a long line of photos along a first-floor wall honoring Frankford Pioneer Alumni of the Year through history. There are scientists, politicians, doctors, military heroes, inventors, scholars, and such, but just one who dropped his college courses to study music for a year, graduated with only a general diploma, and never went to college.

Yes . . . There is just one. The Alumnus of the Year in 1982 . . . Joseph S. Bonsall. 🖊

CHAPTER 64

I had to succeed in music somehow . . . I just HAD to!

I see myself working at the Plumb Tool and Delta File Factories right after I graduated from Frankford High School in June of 1965. My gospel-singing friend Ronnie Graef, who also sang lead in my Faith Four gospel quartet, worked in the mailroom there, and the job was too big for just one guy. So Ronnie talked them into hiring me, and it was quite the experience.

The factory and office buildings were huge, and this company made some of the finest tools around, including the Plumb hammer with Permabond!

It's funny the things you remember. Ronnie and I sorted mail every day and then delivered it as well as office memos to every nook and cranny of the company, which included the heavy steel molding machines which forged the tools. It was very loud with sweaty, shirtless men working their tails off in the hottest temperatures I can ever remember.

By now my dad was stroke-ridden and my mom was working every day at Craftex manufacturing. Between Plumb and my mom and the years of going to a factory with my dad late at night on occasion to fix some piece of machinery that only he could fix, I learned I dang sure didn't want to spend my life working in a factory.

Even after I left Plumb Tools for the National Sugar Refining Company and spent most of my time in a cool office building surrounded by pretty girls, I also knew that working behind a desk wasn't for me either.

College was out of the question, so I had to succeed in music somehow . . . I just HAD to! Only music and singing could get me away from these kinds of jobs and get me away from these concrete sidewalks.

I was willing to work hard every single minute of every single day to make that happen. And even though I didn't really make a decent living at it until I turned thirty years old, my course was set. I was singing songs and traveling with a group and NOT working in a hot factory somewhere in Philadelphia. And I certainly give God the credit for guiding my pathways and giving me just enough talent to get me away from those streets.

As a side note, I worked for Plumb Tool for just about one year and for National Sugar for two years all the while running my little Faith Four quartet up and down the East Coast as far south as the Carolinas and as far north as Maine and as far west as Indiana on most weekends.

I joined the Keystones at age nineteen and would join the Oak Ridge Boys at age twenty-five. All of those years and beyond, everyone I knew kept asking when I was going to get a real job and make a living and, as stated above, it did take some patience and perseverance. But my mother, Lillie, never asked me that question. She was always proud I was following my dream, and she always assured me I would succeed. As usual, my mother was right.

CHAPTER 65

I can still do everything that I have always done, I just move a little slower is all.

I see myself being a bit crippled of late (2022). I have developed a kind of nerve problem in my left leg and foot in the past couple of years and, up until this point, I have had all kinds of nerve tests, MRIs, spinal taps, immunoglobulin infusions (the side effects of which gave me a pulmonary embolism), physical therapy, CT scans, all kinds of bloodwork, and cancer screenings. However, there have been no viable answers.

I may have a very weak leg for the rest of my life or perhaps it still could be a symptom of something worse. Anyhow it is a process to be certain and eventually I will have some answers or perhaps I will not. But rest assured I am not worried about it. I know in my soul that whatever may come, God is in control. It's like I have told my family, it's just a limp, it's not cancer, and it is not a heart issue or anything like that.

Both of my daughters have faced a health issue or two over the years that was much worse than whatever I am dealing with. I can still do everything that I have always done, I just move a little slower is all.

Our bodies are so intricate it is a wonder that something doesn't break every seven minutes—and at my age, my next moments are never guaranteed anyway, so I am good with whatever comes. I have seen all the Oak Ridge Boys deal with a health issue or an injury of some kind over the decades of touring and singing, and I guarantee the audience and even those close to us had no idea that a guy was hurting.

We just keep on singing, and we will keep on singing until God tells us it is over—thus far God has told us in so many ways we are far from over. So if you come to a show these days and notice that tenor boy isn't running across the stage quite like he once did in younger years, just know in your heart I am doing the best I can.

There is nothing wrong with my singing voice so far and that is all that really matters! We had a group text going awhile back that meant the world to me. We were hopefully nearing the end of being shut down by Covid and everyone was anxious to get back to singing, and I mentioned to the guys: *I am trying to be patient, but my heart is saying Let's GO! I may be limping, but I'll be singing!*

I mentioned earlier how deep our Oak Ridge Boys brotherhood and friendship goes, and this text from Duane Allen is the perfect illustration:

> *Joe, you don't need two legs to do what you need to do. You have already worn out most stages we've worked. Just find you a place, get in your comfort zone, and sing your butt off. Your voice is still very strong, and you have done enough running for two lives. Just play the game with what you have. Nobody can do what you have already done. Nobody can equal what you can do with one leg tied behind you. You can use my shoulder for as long as I can stand, and we can help each other off stage. It makes*

me proud to just write this down. At the same time, I am humbled before God that I still have this great pleasure.

WHOA . . . that meant the world! I love the man we call "the Ace"!

CHAPTER 66

"Check Out the Boy Scouts"

I see myself getting kicked out of the Cub Scouts. Okay, I was only ten years old, but I was still a prankster, and I remember my den mother not being able to take it anymore. And I guess I really couldn't blame her.

Our Cub Scout troop would don our navy blue uniforms with our troop number on the sleeve and meet at a Methodist Church on Kensington Avenue just a few blocks away from my house. Overall, I loved being a Cub Scout. There were a bunch of young neighborhood boys just like me, and we learned a lot of cool stuff, including arts and crafts. And we took part in outdoor projects that taught us early elements of survival.

We learned about wildlife and woods and were taught to love America and to respect our elders and to honor God and to make a lanyard. I never knew what to do with a lanyard, but I could make one. These are elements of scouting that do not exist as much now, which is very sad.

I did an incredible imitation of a cartoon character named Quick Draw McGraw and in our most serious moments, especially during prayer I would shout, "HEY BABA LOOOUUUEEEY" and all the kids would bust out laughing.

My alternate imitations were of John Wayne "Wellll Pilgrim" and Mighty Mouse, "UP, UP, AND AWAAAAAYYYYYY."

It came to pass that my den mother—old Mrs. I Don't Remember—began to hate me. It reached a boiling point on a scouting trip to Washington, D.C., when I flipped a forkful of mashed potatoes at her, and it landed right in the middle of her forehead. (I had good aim!)

After the D.C. trip my days of being a Cub Scout were over with no clear path to eventually becoming a Boy Scout. I was good with it though as I would have rather been playing baseball anyway. But fast-forward to the Oak Ridge Boys in 1982 when we became national spokesmen for THE Boy Scouts of America. We would do this for three years and not only shoot commercials and appear at special events in our Boy Scout uniforms, but we also performed at two Boy Scout Jamborees at Fort A.P. Hill, Virginia.

These events were just amazing as thousands upon thousands of young Scouts as far you could see were lighting candles and singing "Elvira." It was truly unforgettable, and I know we did a lot of good for Scouting and for America in those years.

To this day we run into grown up men who saw us sing at one of those Jamborees, and these men are always emotional about it and so are we. Not long ago my U.S. Navy grandson, Luke, was on leave, and he visited Mary and me. Well, for some reason the subject of Scouting came up. I think Luke had seen our "Check Out the Boy Scouts" commercial on YouTube and got a real kick out of seeing a very young Pop-Pop singing in his Boy Scout uniform.

So I told him the whole story about how even though I was kicked out of the Cub Scouts for pranking I eventually became a national spokesman for the Boy Scouts. And at a special dinner in Boston in 2001, I was awarded the Silver Buffalo, which is the highest honor a Scout can receive.

"The Silver Buffalo, man!" I bragged to my grandson, to which my wife added with no break or hesitation, "And he can't even build a campfire!"

CHAPTER 67

Private Joseph S. Bonsall Bronze Star Silver Star Purple Heart
and Corporal Lillie M. Bonsall Women's Army Corps.

I see myself visiting Arlington National Cemetery whenever
possible. A few years back a devastating storm blew through
D.C. the night before we were to do a show in the area. I
sat in the back of the tour bus and watched the pouring rain. I
was so disappointed because I wanted to utilize this day off in
D.C. to visit my parents' graves. At last, around 5 p.m. the skies
cleared, so I decided I still had enough time before dark to make
my way over to Arlington.

The Washington Metro system has a station right there
where I was staying near the Pentagon, and the cemetery was
just two exits down, so away I went. This was an excellent decision because, in the wake of the storm, there was absolutely
nobody there. No funerals were going on, and I only saw one
family of folks walking in another direction far away.

I strolled through the gate near the Women's Memorial and
across the street from the tribute to our Mighty 101st Airborne
Screaming Eagles and began to walk down Eisenhower Avenue
toward York, where my parents' graves lie on that familiar corner
right on the very end of the row beneath a pin oak tree.

The wind was still kicking up through the trees and a few
birds were singing. But other than that, it was all total peace and

respectful silence. It was serene and beautiful and such an honor to be there among the fallen Soldiers and Sailors and Airmen and Marines and Coast Guardsman, who had paid the ultimate price for ALL of us.

After a long visit with Mommy and Daddy, I strolled among the snowy white stones. There were many old veterans like my parents who lived a longer life but carried the scars and burdens of war with them to this final resting place. However, there were also many warriors who left us while still in the youthful prime of their life.

There were so many who had just given their lives, while fighting in Iraq or Afghanistan and other far-away places. Veterans of all wars! Prices paid. Sacrifices made. After a good while, as darkness began to fall, I went back and said farewell to Mommy and Daddy and promised I would return when I could and assured them they were loved and never forgotten.

Private Joseph S. Bonsall, Bronze Star, Silver Star, Purple Heart and Corporal Lillie M. Bonsall Women's Army Corps. I could have stayed there forever listening to the wind and whispers of our nation's heroes, whose remains rest there in the sacred earth while their souls now rest in the Everlasting Arms. But it was time to go, so I walked back to the Metro and rode back to my bus where I thought I might try to attempt to write a few words of inspiration and honor, and you are reading a few of them on this page.

It is hard to put into words how very moved I was during those three hours. I am so thankful God allowed me those moments in space and time to visit them—in the quiet, and all alone. Believe me, we have young men and women who still hear the clarion call to serve and to rise above their own self-interests, and fight for America.

My grandson, Luke, serves in the United States Navy, and I pray for that boy every single day, because I realize there will be more sacrifice and, sadly, there will be more gravestones in Arlington. Because the fight for freedom never ends.

As Christ shed His blood on the cross to forgive us of our sins and provide a way forward, the Patriots who rest here in the bivouac of the dead have also paid the price in blood. May we NEVER forget any of them! Not EVER! ✒

CHAPTER 68

If you really want to see America up close and personal, spend some time on any Saturday afternoon sitting in a Chick-fil-A.

I see myself eating great food or at least the best food I can find on any given day on the road. I always eat great at home because my Mary is a gourmet cook, and when she decides to fire up the kitchen, my dining experience immediately beats anything I would ever be eating on a concert day. Not to say I don't have some favorite eating places around the country—restaurants like Angeloni's in Atlantic City or Vic and Anthony's in Lake Charles or Las Vegas, Taste of Texas in Houston or Rock'n Sushi in Fort Myers, and quite a few others.

But some days it is fun to just go to a fast-food place and people-watch. I recall one such time in Southern Georgia where the Oak Ridge Boys played at a festival in the early afternoon. After the show, I was looking for a place to eat and, quite frankly, in this little town there were very limited choices except for the usual array of fast-food joints.

Thankfully, Chick-fil-A was among them. For me, it's an obvious choice among the McDonalds, Taco Bells, Arby's, and Bojangles of this world. I decided to dine within and ordered my usual chicken noodle soups (*yes* . . . two bowls), a spicy chicken sandwich, and a large unsweetened iced tea.

Taking a seat in the back of the restaurant, I had the pleasure of watching middle America unfold right before my eyes. There were four guys in work clothes talking about what kind of season the Georgia Bulldogs might have in the fall, while debating the merits of handcrafted beer versus any good old American brew. These were working men, the backbone of America.

There was an old couple, around eighty years old or so, who came in holding hands and left holding hands. Very inspiring!

There was a pretty, young blonde girl dressed in the shortest shorts I have ever seen. She seemed totally annoyed that people were staring at her. Well, dang girl, put some clothes on!

There was a table chock-full of teenaged girls all dressed in gothic black, with lots of tattoos and pins in their noses staring deeply into their iPhones and never speaking one word to each other. They just ate and stared. But, in all honesty, they weren't very scary. A bit strange though.

There was a guy at the counter with Rasta locks and a Bob Marley T-shirt who must have been smoking some good weed, because the bag of food he took out to his Cube car was enormous. No problem, Mon!

And the families . . . wow. I saw a young couple with seven kids. There may have been eight, but I am not certain. I don't think they knew for sure either. Then there was a young girl at the counter, who couldn't have been more then twenty-five, but she was toting a set of three-year old twins. She looked more tired than the couple with the herd.

One young couple sitting very close never stopped looking at each other. It appeared that nobody else existed or mattered. Love and spicy chicken were in the air. I wished them well!

Right beside my table, two hunters bragged about how many turkeys they had taken out that week. They were dressed in full camo and, although hunting is perfectly legal, I couldn't help but wonder what it would be like for them if turkeys were able to shoot back. Their attitudes alone made me want to root for the gobblers.

Then several soldiers came in. Now that is REAL camo. The turkeys THEY face DO shoot back. God bless them all!

If you really want to see America up close and personal, spend some time on any Saturday afternoon sitting in a Chick-fil-A. Besides, the food and the service are stellar—and as the cow says, "EAT MOR CHIKIN."

I recall a time while eating in a restaurant in Branson, Missouri, where I came upon two of the most miserable people I ever saw in my life. They did nothing but complain from the time they sat down. The menu was horrible, the waitress was slow, it was too dark in there. On and on it went. They looked to be about eighty years old, give or take a few years on either side.

I wish I could have kept eating my steak and fries and ignored them, but I could not. It's hard not to notice such misery and even harder not to wonder about the root cause.

Now, every life is a story, and everyone has a bit of a dark side, I guess. Some just disguise it better. There had to be a reason. Perhaps they had received some recent bad news. Maybe their son is a serial killer, who just got caught, or maybe they have the shingles. It looked to me like they were in relatively good health, although that is subjective for certain.

What I did observe was they drove up and left in a nice car, and they walked without assistance. They seemed strong mentally—but holy cow, were they miserable. I guarantee if they came to a show, we would be too loud and would sing all the wrong songs.

Heck, they couldn't complain about our appearance much, as we are not that much younger than they are. But I am certain they would have found a lot to moan about. They probably would have asked for their money back because our drummer's hair sticks up in a point!

I guess what seeing folks like this really does, though, is make me think of my mom and dad, who both died way too early from being tired of being sick, and sick of being tired. But they were like a sunrise on the Caribbean compared to these people.

My Lillie would have LOVED to be able to board a tour bus or get in the car with Daddy and drive to a place like Branson, Missouri. She would have LOVED this restaurant and would have treated the waitress like gold no matter how her food was prepared. She would have gone to every show she could and would have probably even ridden the coaster at Silver Dollar City.

Lillie loved everyone, and God knows her scars went deep. I recall a dear sweet old friend, Lo-Dee Hammock, who lost her health in her nineties and never complained—not once! She always smiled and witnessed for Christ and made everyone around her feel welcome and comfortable no matter how she felt.

I remember when her son passed away how very sad she was. But once she emerged from behind her curtain of grief, she made everyone around her feel comfortable with her loss. She cared more about others than she ever did for herself. She inspired me on every level and in every moment of the days I was fortunate enough to know her.

Now, we all have moods—sometimes the dark cloud follows us around for whatever reason and we just can't duck out from under it. I am not being judgmental here. It is just that these two folks made me sad—sad for THEM!

Maybe they only need more God in their lives! Maybe they are tired of each other's company. I did notice he walked out ahead of her and did NOT open the car door for her. He just slid behind the wheel and started the car while grumbling about who knows what. Maybe she has been tired of his crap for decades and hates his guts, or maybe she had an affair with the landscape guy in 1976, and he has never forgiven her. Who knows?

I DO know this: whatever is bringing you down, Jesus Christ can and WILL lift you up. There is never a reason to mistreat people, and an occasional smile is actually very good for you. I hope and pray I read them wrong, and I really wish them a better time of it all. But my gift of discernment rarely lets me down, and this couple seemed to be on a very negative and unhappy pathway—and at a certain age, there is not all that much pathway left. As for me, I am thankful for the Lillies and Lo-Dees of this world who have influenced my own pathway. Just thinking of them makes me smile and makes any dark cloud in my own life vanish as if it never existed in the first place.

CHAPTER 69

"Here's what we would like for you to consider . . ." I knew I didn't want anything to do with this stuff.

I see myself colliding with the Mafia while singing with the Keystones in Buffalo, New York. It was perhaps the scariest and most harrowing story of my life. I received a phone call out of the clear blue one night in my apartment in Kenmore, New York, from a man who said he represented the Magaddino Funeral Home and invited me to a private dinner—he would not take no for an answer.

Now anyone with any sense at all knew the Magaddino crime family ruled Western New York in those days and the funeral home was a front for all kinds of mob business. I'll admit, I was more than apprehensive about the whole thing, but I sheepishly agreed I would attend.

The restaurant was a nice little Italian joint, and when I arrived the maître d' seated me at a table in the back. I was joined by two men who looked more like businessmen than mob guys, but my Spidey-sense was still working overtime.

They were very nice and polite, making a lot of small talk about the Keystones and gospel music and concerts we had promoted. I was becoming more and more nervous because these guys just seemed to know *too much* about me. Then they dropped the expected bomb.

"How much money do you make?" one guy asked.

"Around $150 a week on most weeks, sometimes less," I answered timidly.

"Well, you can do much better than that. Here's what we would like for you to consider. Whenever your singing group crosses into Canada in that big bus, we want you to take some stuff across the border for us, and when you return, we would like for you to bring some stuff back to us. It's very simple, we will handle the logistics and all you need to do is hide some packages on that bus, and in so doing you will start making a lot more money than you are now. A LOT more! We'll get back to you."

Just like that, they got up and exited the restaurant, leaving me staring at what was left of my veal piccata. Remember, I was just twenty-three years old at the time, married, living in a dinky apartment, and starving to death. But I knew I didn't want anything to do with any of this stuff. So I called an old preacher friend of mine down near Pittsburgh, Pennsylvania, by the name of Domenick Sgro.

Now Reverend Sgro had a small church in the McKeesport area, and I first met him when he booked the Faith Four to sing in his church, and we became great friends right off. In later years the Keystones would sing there often, and on those occasions, after Sister Sgro would cook up a nice dinner after the service, Brother Sgro and I would sit for hours and share stories.

I would tell him all about my parents and growing up in Philly and how I came to know Jesus as my Savior, and he would share with me the most amazing stories of being a part of the Cleveland, Ohio, mob in his younger days. Well, Domenick got saved and felt the call to preach, and they allowed him to leave the crime family with the warning he was to never talk about them ever.

So after my dinner with the Magaddino guys, Domenick Sgro's wise counsel was for me to just lay low and he would make some calls and take care of it. And that is just what he did, because I never heard from the Buffalo mob ever again.

I would join the Oak Ridge Boys and move to Nashville in just a few years. Even though I was a big fan of the Buffalo Bills and Sabres, I was not only thrilled to be joining the Oaks, but I was just as thrilled to get away from the Niagara Frontier.

As a side note, I stayed close to Dom Sgro until he passed in 2016. I loved him dearly, and he loved Joey Bonsall. He always told me he would be there for me anytime and anyplace, and he certainly proved it.

Thank you, sir, for being at the crossroads at a time when I really needed you. I have never forgotten. 🎤

CHAPTER 70

When you see me onstage singing Christmas songs with the Oak Ridge Boys, perhaps you will now realize how deep the river runs. I love Christmas.

I see myself loving Christmas. Every night during our massive, yearly Christmas tour, about halfway through every show we roll out a beautiful fireplace and a fully decorated Christmas tree complete with four Cracker Barrel Old Country Store rocking chairs. Then all four Oak Ridge Boys sit and rock and chat about memories of Christmas past and sing a few favorite songs to the gathered crowd.

It has become a very popular part of our Christmas show. Much like in this book, I enjoy chatting about growing up in Philadelphia and mentioning how my mother always taught me that if I was honest, worked hard, told the truth, and honored God in my life, I could do anything I wanted to do and be anything I wanted to be because this was America. Then she would point over at Daddy sitting in his wheelchair and add, "That's why guys like him did what they did, so don't blow it!"

Mommy was right. And maybe if we had more parents like her encouraging their children to be the best they can be, our world would be a better place. Lillie was the ultimate person standing at my crossroads.

I have so many great Christmas memories. My parents would always make Christmas morning special for me and my sister, Nancy. Whatever we asked for was usually under the tree, although our family didn't have a lot of means. The tree, the platform, the lights, the Lionel train, and the presents were there because Mommy and Daddy worked extra jobs to provide for us. My mom would work three jobs in December just to pay for Christmas.

I see myself every Thanksgiving with my parents who took us kids to the Gimbels Thanksgiving Day Parade in downtown Philly. Gimbels was a big department store, and they went all out, as did Lit Brothers and John Wanamaker's, who made their stores look like Disneyland during the season.

None of those stores are around today and that is sad. My mom always told me the Santa Claus who appeared in the Gimbels parade was indeed the REAL Santa and that all the others were his helpers. That included any Santa on the street ringing a bell and even the Macy's Santa in New York! They were ALL helpers.

The real Santa visited Philadelphia and at the end of the parade he would rise out of his sleigh, climb up a huge fire truck ladder several stories high, and then vanish through a Gimbels window right into the toy department! There he would hold court with thousands of children from Thanksgiving Day right on through Christmas Eve.

Santa climbing that ladder with his bag slung over his shoulder was one of the greatest sights a little Philly boy could witness, and I can still see it clearly in my mind's eye. Since I was fortunate enough to have the real Santa just a subway ride away from my house, I believed that when I asked him for a Rin Tin Tin Fort Apache set or a bow and arrow that I would receive it.

And I always did. Nancy and I tried not to ask for very much as we were taught, but Santa always came through.

One year, Nancy asked for a Patti Playpal doll, and on Christmas morning there it was. She cried with joy for over an hour.

I see myself gazing at the little manger scene resting beneath the tree. It was illuminated by one small white bulb, making it seem like Baby Jesus was lit up more than Joseph or Mary or the animals. I can still see the angel at the top of the tree all lit up beautifully. It was the same angel every year. I loved that angel.

It was also the same lights and balls every year as well. Only the tinsel was new, and my mother was very generous with the tinsel. Thank God it was fireproof, because it was everywhere! I see the big wooden platform that Daddy built. He would put it up on Christmas Eve, and I just never knew how he ever got that thing up and out of the cellar on his own, but he did.

He would put an entire miniature city, complete with people and buildings and a train and a tunnel on that platform. It was wondrous!

My parents did all of this on Christmas Eve, while we slept upstairs in our room. When we went up to bed, the living room was as it always was. But when Nancy and I came down the stairs the next morning, it was as if a magic wand had been waved—a complete transformation!

After Daddy had his stroke and spent several years in VA hospitals, he came back to us at last. And for his first Christmas home, some of my buddies and I put up the old platform. It took four of us to get that thing upstairs from the basement. I remember my father weeping like a baby over that platform.

The bottom line is this: When you see me onstage singing Christmas songs with the Oak Ridge Boys, perhaps you will now realize how deep the river runs. I love Christmas. I have tried to make it just as magical for my family as when Joey and Nancy descended those stairs on Jasper Street all those years ago.

Thank you, Mommy and Daddy. Most of these Christmas memories will never fade. So Merry Christmas, everyone! Remember that the same Jesus who was born in the manger on that First Christmas Day is the same Jesus who can solve your problems and guide your life today. All you need is to believe in Him and then learn to lean upon Him!

This crazy world twists and turns and changes constantly, but Jesus never changes. He is the same yesterday, today, and tomorrow!

CHAPTER 71

It is amazing to me how people can remember where they were when they first heard "Elvira."

I see myself singing "Elvira"! In the spring of 2021, we sang Happy FORTIETH Birthday to our favorite girl. It is so hard to believe it has now been well over those forty years since the entire nation was singing this Dallas Frazier–penned song with the Oak Ridge Boys.

It was an amazing time for us in 1981—after five gold albums, lots of number-one hit records, a monumental tour with Kenny Rogers, and tons of awards, we were about to accelerate into super stardom just because of this fun little song.

Now I believe that songs and music in general mark space and time better than anything else—except for perhaps baseball—and it is amazing to me how people can remember where they were when they first heard "Elvira." I give our producer, Ron Chancey, all the credit in the world for his leadership and studio genius in the matter. We were working on our album called *Fancy Free* near the end of 1980, and we were about to wrap it all up when an Acuff Rose Music Publishing Company song plugger and friend, Ron Gant, came into the Woodland Sound Studio and presented the idea to record "Elvira." He had heard some bar band sing it on a trip to Texas, and a light went on: *The Oak Ridge Boys could nail this song to the wall!*

And so he brought the idea to Ron Chancey, who figured, "Well, it is unlike anything else on this project so maybe we can give it a shot."

The four of us have always been open to new ideas, and we are still wide open to new creative ideas today. Look up our version of the White Stripes song, "Seven Nation Army" produced by now legendary producer Dave Cobb to illustrate that fact. Our attitude was, "It sounds like fun, so let's do it!"

I think we sang through "Elvira" just two or three times. I pretty much fooled around on the verses, and Richard became the most famous bass singer in the world with his vocal treatment of the *oom papa mau mau's*. And the rest is music history.

How big can one song get? It can become bigger than one could ever possibly imagine, After forty-plus years, the Oak Ridge Boys are still singing "Elvira" and people *still* want to hear it.

When I shout out "Let's Sing 'ELVIRA!'" near the end of a show, the audience rises as one, as if we were singing the "Hallelujah Chorus." And they still sing every single word right along with us. Hopefully we will still be singing "Elvira" for many more years to come . . . "High ho Silver, away!"

Let us look at 1981: Ronald Reagan was in the first year of his presidency, the internet was still five years away, cable TV was in its infancy, nobody had a personal computer unless it was a Commodore Vic-64—in fact, the Apple Macintosh was still three more years away, so there was no smart phone glued to our faces either. We were listening to music on vinyl records and cassettes because the compact disc didn't arrive until the next year, 1982.

The biggest songs of the day were Rick Springfield singing about "Jessie's Girl," Kim Carnes going on about "Bette Davis Eyes," Kool & The Gang having a "Celebration," and "Elvira" by you know who! Our little song won every single music award given for 1981 from a Grammy to the CMA, ACM, and BMI—and even the Jukebox Award. Yes, there were even jukeboxes in 1981!

Had the FBI or CIA given out music awards back then, "Elvira" would have won them. If you were a little kid, then or perhaps even now, "Elvira" just might have been the first song you ever learned to sing.

CHAPTER 72

The creative process—something that exists today that was not here yesterday because you followed a vision or an idea. Everyone has the ability and the capacity to create.

I see myself writing and trying to come up with pages of simple prose that people might find interesting enough to read—perhaps a paragraph or two that might influence the reader with a certain positivity to even be life-changing. I have been blessed with having ten books published, and I also have lots of work that has been turned down, or unfinished, or just deemed by my own self not to be very good.

Writing articles or books is much like writing songs. I haven't written many songs, but on a rare occasion God has blessed me with a song that moved hearts. "G.I. Joe and Lillie" and "Sacrifice" are two that come to mind. But trust me, I have an entire file of mediocre songs the public will never hear, and that is a good thing.

I see myself writing an entire novel called *Whitetail Hollow* about a protagonist named John Barlow who, after the terrorist attack on 9/11/01, became a secret warrior in the fight against terror. He was the best there was at leading a light attack unit into bad situations and winning for America, all the while juggling a family life and maintaining his faith in God. I took so long working on this book over the years that it all became a bit outdated. I am still proud of the work, but I am doubtful it will ever come out.

I have a Civil War–era time travel romance novel about half written, and I would say that some of it is pretty good, but it lives in a drawer with my book about country music singing cats. Johnny Cat, Minnie Purr, Blake Shedding, and a bunch of other street cats who perform weekly at the Litter Box Café and fight off evil Dog rappers. Trust me, publishers laughed hard at that one, so it is doubtful this little book will ever see the light of day.

However, the biggest enemy of any writer is the blank page. The blank page stares back at every creative writer who has ever lived. Whether a screenwriter, author, lyricist, or poet, the purveyor of words sometimes stares into the abyss of emptiness and waits for that story idea or special rhyme that can touch his or her own soul enough to pursue the given course and later to perhaps touch others with the prose of it all.

Throughout time the writer has stared and prayed, or at the very least hoped for, those special life-changing words of inspiration. The ancients no doubt gazed at an empty scroll of papyrus and waited in the same manner with quill in hand as I sometimes peer at a blank page of word processing software on my laptop.

For the writer, trashcans are filled with attempts to jot down a beginning story line or the bridge of a good song. *The night was dark* . . . no . . . *The azure-colored morning light appeared to* . . . no . . . *I took her in my arms and* . . . NO! The crumpled page, the deleted page, the frustration—yet all the while knowing down deep the words would eventually come as they always do, so we keep staring and praying and churning and dreaming . . . and writing.

That first line is oh so important. Open a well-written, successful book, and I assure you the first line is spell-binding. The same goes for a song: "He Stopped Loving Her Today," recorded by George Jones and written by Bobby Braddock and Curly Putman. Check it out. Point made.

In the mid-nineties I bought my first laptop and headed off for a two-week stint in Las Vegas, leaving my family and a wonderful little kitten named Molly behind. I was anxious to write something on my new Mac, and I stared at a blank page and finally wrote, "Molly was two years old although she still looked somewhat like a kitten. It is just that she never grew very big." *Whoa*, I thought, *I have a good start here*, and away I went writing more successfully about talking cats than I ever did about singing cats.

But folks, I seriously believe that everyone has a creative talent. A book, a blog, a song, or perhaps a newly designed kitchen countertop or a new recipe for shrimp scampi. It's called the creative process—something that exists today that was not here yesterday because you followed a vision or an idea.

Everyone has the ability and the capacity to create. Many of us are just not in tune with the process. God can help you with this because . . . let's face it, He is indeed the Great Creator, and all thoughts and ideas began with Him. We just need to be listening.

Write on! 🎤

CHAPTER 73

I know down deep in my heart I will NEVER come back to
Jasper Street . . . ever again.

I see myself going back to Philadelphia just a few times since
my parents left Jasper Street. I wrote much of the following
piece the year before they passed, and it seemed to fit in with
much of the thought process behind this book so here it is.

The Oak Ridge Boys had a day off in Hershey, Pennsylvania, so I rented a Toyota Corolla at the Harrisburg
airport and drove across the countryside to the little
town of Spring City. This is the home of the Southeastern Pennsylvania Veterans Center where my mom and
dad, both veterans of World War II, now reside. It was a
bright and sunny spring afternoon, and I was so happy
my concert schedule allowed me to see my folks.

Usually, a day off is spent in some town a long way
off with nothing to do but take a walk and watch the
corn grow, however today everything worked out just
right. I parked the rental car in the main lot and proceeded to the fourth floor of the Veterans Center. Mom
was upbeat as usual, and Dad was downbeat as usual,
although I cannot blame him. His old stroke-ridden
body is so frail now and, besides that, he just had a toe

removed and he is in pain from a bout with the shingles. Otherwise, I guess he is doing just great!

I took my mom out to dinner and to a Walmart, which was a big day for her. I bought a few new blouses for her, and I bought Daddy a singing fish called Billy Bass or something goofy like that. Anyhow, it sang "Don't Worry, Be Happy," and he laughed so hard that he almost fell out of bed. Well worth the $22.50 for a singing fish.

I said goodbye to them both and headed into the City of Brotherly Love.

It is late afternoon as I exit the Schuylkill Expressway and turn on to U.S. Route 1 North. I notice the sun is just now beginning to sink behind William Penn's hat on top of City Hall in center Philadelphia.

I chuckle at this point. The statue of Penn on top of City Hall collects rainwater in a storm, and it drains off the hat in such a way that if you stand on South Broad Street and look up, Mr. Penn appears to be taking a hearty, colonial piss on downtown Philly. I swear it is true. Check it out sometime. I needed that light moment.

The Veterans Center is a wonderful facility, and my folks are truly, very well taken care of there. Their years of service to this country and all the medals hanging over Daddy's bed have earned them the right to that care, and for that I am very appreciative. However, seeing them there somehow rips my heart into little pieces, and it takes days to push it all back a bit farther into my mind.

Their last several years of living in the old house had become very scary, and I worried about them constantly. Even though I had a state-of-the-art (I hate that expression) security system installed, and even though my sister, Nancy, lived relatively close in nearby Cherry Hill, New Jersey, the streets were getting worse and the whole neighborhood was going downhill faster every day.

Also, Mom's diabetes was getting worse. Her eyesight was failing and after a diabetic coma hit her and we almost lost her, it was time to talk serious turkey. Mom agreed and led the way (as usual) to make plans for what she called the "Soldiers Home."

They have lived in the Soldiers Home for two years now. One year ago today, Nancy sold the little row house my parents had lived in for fifty years. Little Joey Bonsall grew up in that house and now I am driving there, and I am not even sure why I am doing it.

Anyhow, I exit the Roosevelt Expressway and take a left onto Wingohocking Street. I have always chuckled at that too. Such a funny name: "Wingohocking Street Exit 1/4 mile." I am so glad I never lived on that street. On to Hunting Park Avenue. That sounds much better. *Oh, you live by Hunting Park. Oh my. Well, well! How very nice.*

Yeah, right!

I pass through the new Spanish-speaking complex of row houses right off Hunting Park where the music is pounding out of the passing cars so loudly the street is shaking. When I was sixteen and jacked up the volume on my cheesy-sounding radio in my old winged monster '59 Impala, people would yell at me from their front porches to "turn that thing down"—or off! (I was probably only blasting "Soldier Boy" by the Shirelles.)

Nowadays, kids have badass rap music thumping out of bass speakers from hell, with lyrics about rape and killing, and people are just too afraid to say anything about it. Ah, the whiff of passing and changing times . . . It is not always a pleasant aroma.

I make my way through all of that without getting shot or taken hostage, and I am still quite a few blocks from my old house. I drive through a neighborhood called Juniata. It is just another several blocks of row houses, but the homes on these streets always seemed a little nicer, more well-kept with little bitty lawns with a few azalea bushes and awnings on the windows. When I was little, I used to think that moving about fifteen blocks over to Juniata would really be moving on up.

I remember when the Williamson family over on Clearance Street moved over there, taking two rather good-looking daughters with them—Janet and Diane Williamson might as well have been moving to a new row house on the moon.

What everyone really dreamed about was moving to a home on the Jersey Shore. When I was a kid, that was the goal of the hard-working people in the old neighborhood. To live down at "da shore"! Atlantic City, Wildwood, Ocean City, Cape May . . . Hey, it really didn't matter. Just to live at da shore by the ocean.

I don't believe I ever saw the Williamson girls again after their big move to Juniata. I never remember anyone ever moving to da shore either. I drive on through Juniata, down K Street to Kensington Avenue. Ah, getting close. I cross Kensington and go under the El.

The Elevated Frankford Commuter Train was called "the El" when it ran above ground and "the subway" when it ran beneath the ground. That seemed to always make sense, and one thing that did not change was the sound of the El pulling into the Tioga Street station just one block from where I grew up. I pulled over and listened. The sound of those iron wheels on the tracks as they slow to a halt was indeed a sound of childhood and, hey, they have even remodeled the old station.

When I was a kid, the Tioga Street El station was where bums hung out. They are called homeless now, I guess. But back then we called them bums, and they are the reason the old El station smelled like stale pee.

On a hot, muggy summer day—YO, it was rough. I'll bet the new station still smells a little like pee. You could get on that train and go right on into downtown Philly or go the other way and end up in Frankford where I went to high school. Either way, you held your nose while digging for a token.

On a musical note, the El station had great acoustics. Guys would gather down there and sing harmony. We all sounded good as our voices echoed off the walls and the bums seemed to really enjoy it. By now, you have noticed that each inner-city neighborhood has its own name, and each has its own personality and identity as well.

This city is really made up of small towns that are entities all unto themselves with names like Fishtown, Kensington, Frankford, Harrowgate, Mayfair. As a teenager I was involved in some big fights defending the local turf. Basically, the young guys all fought for

Kensington because our Harrowgate area was a part of Kensington.

The main intersection was Kensington and Allegheny Avenues, which was three blocks from the Tioga El station. There was an Allegheny Avenue El station as well, and it also smelled like pee. I used to think it was so funny that guys would get so bent out of shape over a few concrete streets. We were much like alley cats staking out our territory.

I always figured, however, if war were to ever break out between Philly and say, Trenton, New Jersey, or Baltimore or maybe even Camden, that all these guys would gather as one big army and march down Interstate 95 wearing Phillies' hats and Eagles' helmets shouting "YO!" and eating cheesesteaks and soft pretzels.

Anyhow, I grew up on Jasper Street, which was right by Harrowgate Square. The little park was looked over by the City Department of Recreation, and I mean, just that. The city would mow around the War World II Memorial on the Kensington Avenue side from time to time, but for the most part, it was just looked over.

Neighborhood folks just called it "da square." It was just one square block of grass, trees, and dog poop. But to little boys like my Blackhawks, it became a ballpark or a football stadium or even a boxing ring with just a slight turn of the imagination.

Each neighborhood had its own string band, and the Harrowgate String Band was one of the best in the city. On a rare occasion, they would put on a concert in da square, and everybody would come out to hear them. These bands were a very strange phenomenon and remain a part of Philly folklore to this day. The bands were made up of average neighborhood guys who would dress up in feathered outfits and play old songs like "Oh, Dem Golden Slippers," while drinking whiskey from a hip flask. Each New Year's Day these string bands from all over the Delaware Valley would gather to march and dance through downtown Philly in front of thousands of people and a nationwide TV audience. It is still a huge event that is called the Mummers Parade, which is kind of like a weird Mardi Gras for guys who hang out in bars.

Guys who would knock your block off at an Eagles' game would dress up in purple feathers and funny pointed shoes and enthusiastically play the living daylights out of banjos and xylophones, while doing a silly dance called the Mummers Strut as they marched down Market Street. There is even a Mummers Hall of Fame. All of this, mind you, from the same city that gave us *American Bandstand*.

So I drive on under the El across Kensington Avenue, and proceed one block down Venango Street to Jasper and turn right. I slowly drive past three small blocks of row houses, garages, alleyways, and trash, and pull over to the curb and park directly across the street from the old house that built me, as Miranda Lambert would sing. I roll down the driver's side window and just sit there.

To my right is a vacant corner lot piled with trash that was once Del's Restaurant, where actual mob guys used to eat. It was amazing! At lunchtime there would be Cadillacs and Lincolns parked on the street where normally there were just Fords and Chevys belonging to the blue-collar working men who lived in these homes. Now old Del's was torn down and all that was left was a pile of rat-infested rubbish.

A few years before, I had taken part in the Presidents' Summit on Volunteerism program that was held right here in Philly. The Oak Ridge Boys and former President George H. W. Bush went into a section called Germantown and cleaned up a few streets with the help of a bunch of nice city kids. Presidents, generals, and volunteers spread out across Philadelphia to clean up the streets and inspire people to keep them clean, to volunteer, and to be a mentor to young people.

It was a great event, and I believe that a lot of good took place. However, they missed this section of Harrowgate, one block from Kensington and the El, and they sure as heck missed old Del's corner.

I sit in my rented Corolla and stare over at the two-story home at 3517 Jasper Street. I would like to say the sinking sun was shining on the second floor and there were happy faces of young children playing on the porch, while Mom cooked salisbury steak and Dad showered the grease off from the factory while smoking a Winston. (I had to say that as my father always smoked a cigarette while taking a bath.)

But no, none of these things were happening. The house was all shut up and dark and still looked pretty much the same as the day when Nancy and I loaded G.I. Joe and Lillie into an ambulance for their last ride down Jasper Street on their way to the Soldiers Home.

In my mind's eye, I could see Joey sitting inside the enclosed porch with Mommy and dear old Nana Clark.

I could see my sister posing in her brand-new Easter
dress. I could see Daddy's latest brand-new, used car
parked by the telephone pole.

I could see a young teenage Joey sitting on the
corner of what was then Flannery's candy store with
about eight other guys, who were just as energetic and
confused as he was. I see a boy running down the street
all bloodied up from a fistfight he lost and trying hard
not to cry.

I see a young Lillie standing on the corner yelling
over toward Harrowgate Park, "Joeeeyyyyy!" at the top
of her lungs, hoping for a response from the dirty little
kid wearing a Phillies' hat and playing baseball. I saw
my father park his Studebaker and then—thanks to a
good mix of Seagram's 7 and Ballantine beer—not be
able to get out of it and walk to the house. So he stayed
in the car and slept while his dinner got cold.

I see Joey on his bike riding through the streets
searching the bars for Daddy, and when he found him,
he would ride back and tell his mother where he was
and then several neighborhood men would gather and
go to that bar, pick him up, and bring him home. As
I sit here, these images and mirages constantly appear
and fade like an episode of *The Twilight Zone*.

Strangely enough, my whole thought pattern is
interrupted by some goofy girl in a white miniskirt with
purple lips, multi-colored hair, and pins in her nose.
She is pounding on the passenger side window and
saying something.

I roll the window down to hear these pearls of
wisdom: "Hey, are ya dating?" she asked.

I almost break out laughing.

"Hey, you're not a cop, are ya?"

That is even funnier, an old cop in an Avis rental Corolla. Now, that would really have been undercover! Then, I notice the five guys not far behind her watching our every move. It scares me a bit, however—I kind of feel like jumping out of this stupid-looking little gray car and kicking some honest-to-God, old-time, Philly ass!

This old neighborhood was far from perfect when I grew up here. The families who occupied these little row homes had their share of trouble and ours was no exception. Some worked in various factories. Some were truck drivers, policemen, and firemen and such. They were all tough, blue-collar guys who drank and smoked too much. Most of them fought in the wars from Normandy to Iwo Jima to Korea, and they still maintained at least some sort of pride in themselves.

June Cleaver didn't live here either. However, I remember so many wonderful mothers like my own, who worked extra jobs to help make ends meet, and raised families and did the best they could. I see couples smoking cigarettes and playing canasta sitting around our dining room table. They would all smoke and drink a beer or two except for my mother who would send me on up the block to the Shamrock Bar to pick up some roast beef on weck sandwiches and maybe some shrimp baskets, and when I arrived home with the food, she would ask me to sing a few songs for the gathered friends after they were finished playing cards. And, of course, being the little hambone that I was, I would stand there and sing my brains out.

Yes, I grew up here, and I learned a lot of harsh lessons and, quite honestly, I was learning a few more on this day. That old phrase "everything changes, everything stays the same" does not apply to the corner of Jasper and Tioga. Nothing here is the same! Flannery's candy store, Elmer's hardware, Russock's drug store, Mrs. Tuma's dry cleaning, and Emrich's grocery store are long gone. Progress Manufacturing, Craftex Textiles, Schlicter's Steel Mill, Crown Can Company, and many others have long since been boarded up. The Midway and Iris Theaters have been replaced by a McDonalds and a bail bond establishment.

Don't get me wrong, I know in my heart that there are still a lot of good, honest, hardworking people around here who—like the generations before them—are also doing the best they can. It is just that I wonder if the dreams are still there. I hope so.

I once walked these streets with a head and heart full of dreams and plans and goals I would someday accomplish. I went sidewise a few times, but I never lost sight of my future. Where are the dreams of this young hooker and these hard-bodied thugs behind her, smoking pot and listening to loud, crappy music!

The trash in the streets speaks volumes about lost pride, and I find it all very sad and depressing. However, a voice screams out inside of my heart, thanking my Almighty God for the Veterans Center and for His constant, guiding hand on my life all these years.

A wave of common sense prevails, and I do not jump out of the car.

"I gotta go," I tell the young street girl as the neighborhood darkens. "Why don't you guys clean up around here a little!" I yell as I lay serious Toyota rubber on Jasper Street!

Whoa, big tough Philly boy. I am laughing again.

I used to think I could move back to the city anytime, and I guess I could if I had to. However, it would have to be a Supreme Court decision or a burning bush experience to ever pry me away from the rolling hills of Tennessee.

I drive over the Betsy Ross Bridge and have dinner with my wonderful sister in Jersey. We were always such a small ship—Mom, Dad, Nancy, and me—and I love my sister so very much. In fact, I love her more than ever.

"Went by the old house on the way here."

"Neighborhood is awful isn't it," she replies.

"Why did Mommy stay there so long? God knows I tried to get her to move out for years," I said.

"Old school, Joey. You know that. She worked hard and—"

"IT WAS PAID OFF!" We said it in perfect unison, while laughing out loud.

Nancy made me a wonderful dinner. We laughed and cried and said goodbye. I drove in the darkness for three hours back toward Chocolate Town and the Oak Ridge Boys and sang songs. Old rock and roll songs, some Springsteen, and a few gospel tunes. I sang so hard that I really didn't have much voice left for the show the next night.

By two a.m., I was back in a Hershey hotel room, tucked hard into bed and dreaming about hitting a baseball over the park benches in our make-believe

Connie Mack Stadium at Harrowgate Square. The black electrical tape around the old ball makes it hard to find as dusk settles, and the tree branches start to meld in with the sky. I circle the bases, laughing. A tree is first base, second base is a mound of dirt, third is a light pole, and home plate is a strategically placed paper bag. I stomp hard on the bag and my mother's voice fills the air. "Joeeeeyyyy, come on home and eat! Your father and Nancy are already at the table." She sounds a little like Lucille Ball in my dream.

"Coming MAAAAAAA!" I yell as I pick up my old Adirondack bat and my Jimmy Piersall model Wilson glove, and head across Tioga Street toward home. Old Del is sweeping leaves off his sidewalk and waves at me as I cross the street and disappear inside of that two-story row house on 3517 Jasper Street.

My old city is a lot rougher now than it ever was in my teen years or even at the time of the above visit. I remember the dark days of the late sixties quite well. Those were hard times, but now things seem worse than ever as kids are shooting each other, and destructive behavior, vandalism, and crime have become almost tolerated as police departments are being defunded in the name of social justice.

The homeless problems and the drug problems are rampant now, and a new skid row has appeared within blocks of where I grew up. I have watched my old neighborhood go from West Side Story, where a bunch of troubled boys sat on street corners and fought and bullied their way through life to much worse. Now gangs and drugs and cartels rule Kensington.

Those streets where Nana Clark and I walked and shopped together are now filled with ragged tents and sad souls overdosing on heroin and other opioids. There are trash and needles and even dead bodies everywhere. It all looks like a very bad movie is being filmed there, except it is really happening.

This is sad because I know down deep in my heart I will NEVER come back to Jasper Street . . . ever again.

CHAPTER 74

Dreaming is as much a part of my life as breathing and singing, and I have experienced all three since childhood. I breathe. I sing. I dream!

I see myself dreaming. Dreams have always been a part of my life. I actually dreamed about how I would write this book. The very words *I See Myself* came to me in a dream about blue people. I woke up that morning and started to write.

Dreams themselves are a very strange phenomenon. Whether they be pleasant or sexual in nature or downright scary, it is a fact of life that our subconscious can conjure up some very unusual imaginings.

To me dreaming is as much a part of my life as breathing and singing, and I have experienced all three since childhood. I breathe. I sing. I dream!

Sometimes I think dreams may indeed be visions from God, but I don't know for certain. I do know dreams can inspire creativity. Many times, you may see something in a dream which inspires you in some way. Perhaps a song or a story idea can be taken from a dream, but you must write it down quickly before it evaporates. I have forgotten most all my deep sleep dreams save for a few, which have recurred enough times over the years that I have been forced to pay attention to them.

I once dreamed over and over about being in a prison camp in Viet Nam. I found myself handcuffed to a seat in an old school bus when a uniformed enemy soldier enters the bus and puts a gun to my head. A voice from somewhere says, "Oh just kill him," and he squeezes the trigger!

I always wake up in a cold sweat. Yes, I have had this same dream over and over since my forties and have always found it disconcerting. Although, to be honest, this dream has not reoccurred in some time for which I am very thankful.

We always try to analyze or even over-analyze these things— usually to no avail. There are supposed dream interpreters out there, but I think most of these people are full of beans. Not to say there are not a few gifted seers around. I have just never met one except an old piano-playing, songwriting friend of mine named Garland Craft, who always did seem to have some decent vision into the unknown.

However, his own nights were always fitful and full of nightmares. He often dreamed a glowing, red-eyed being was trying to catch him. That always made for some scary evenings on a tour bus when your keyboard guy begins to scream at the top of his lungs! The man we called the Big G always seemed to have an interpretation though. And, on some occasions, he seemed to have it all figured out.

He did . . . I did NOT!

Anyhow, I love dreams about flying—except it can turn dark awfully fast when you cannot seem to land, and you keep rising higher and higher.

I have dreamed I was on a Ferris wheel and as we approach the apex, I keep on rising leaving the county fair, or whatever, far below. I always wake up scared to death and feeling helpless at my inability to come back down to earth.

By the same token I have had some wonderful dreams about flying above the streets in a big city, whizzing by skyscrapers— probably inspired by Spiderman!

We all dream about falling, right? Urban legends have told us since childhood if you land in one of those falls you die! Thankfully, we usually wake with a start and a jump while in the middle of a free fall and scare the living daylights out of our spouse and whichever cat (or cats) is sharing the bed at the time!

Speaking of my spouse, my Mary has nightmares many nights. In her dreams someone or something is usually chasing her. When I am home I try to gently awaken her before the entity grabs hold of her. I think most of her dreams are grounded in the fact that she watches tons of ghost shows all the time. Our DVR is a hoot! Ghost stories here, a haunting there, celebrity ghosts, and even animal ghosts. Mix in a few UFOs and Sasquatch sightings, and it's no wonder she has nightmares.

I do hate it though when I am away on tour and not there to gently wake her and rescue her from a Bigfoot. But the big dream catcher over her bed surely protects her when I am away, right? *RIGHT?*

Even animals dream. It is always fun to watch our cats dream. Perhaps in their kitty dreams they are a cheetah and just brought down a wildebeest or something. By the same token, a puppy may be running with wolves as he howls and his paws run in place.

I had a doozy of a dream that came to me just one time, but I never forgot it. I have played it repeatedly in my mind until I am forced to put a pen to paper and write about it. If you are still with me thus far in my musings, here goes—fasten your seatbelt, please, for it is a strange and bumpy ride . . .

The dream begins in a bowling alley—which is strange enough to begin with as I have not bowled in years—yet there we were in the far lane against the wall. Mary and I, and our two grandchildren, Breanne and Luke, were taking turns competing, and I know I was losing because I am a terrible bowler. My highest game ever is a 145 and, man, did the stars line up for that one. My average is like 105—maybe.

Our daughters, Jennifer and Sabrina, were two lanes over chatting with Taylor Swift and her mom and dad. Now that image is easy to figure as I had just spent time with Taylor and her folks after her show in Dallas. The strange thing was that my granddaughter Breanne, who just adores Taylor, was not paying any attention to her at all. Instead, she rolled a perfect strike as everyone cheered.

Someone spoke to me about something weird appearing on my shoulder and, sure enough, there on my left shoulder was a growth of some kind. It seemed gooey and smelled horrible. I was wearing a red, woolen pullover sweater—which I would never be wearing in the first place—and the smell of this thing on my shoulder kept getting worse and worse. As everyone started to back away, I quickly pulled the sweater up and over my head.

It all gets quite nightmarish for a bit now, so I am going to get a bit Stephen King on you. However, I promise it won't last long.

When the sweater came off, I saw my entire body decaying, and the smell was downright nauseating. My lungs were oozing through my ribcage and my liver was black and had already hit the floor. I will not elaborate anymore . . . you get the picture.

Next came a searing pain like I could never have imagined. I screamed out. I could not believe I was hurting this bad. It was like someone had taken a cattle prod to every single nerve ending in my body from my teeth to my toes, and I was mercifully starting to pass out when suddenly I was being carried upward while under the arm of what had to be an angel.

It seemed like a feminine presence, but I was just not sure. I whispered, "The pain is gone." My voice seemed distant and not my own.

"All pain is gone now," answered the Being. I heard the voice inside my mind as opposed to audibly.

"Am I dead?" I asked.

"You have simply left the former," she or it replied.

I thought I was probably dead for sure and that thought brought me no discomfort whatsoever. I seemed like someone else now. All things Joseph Bonsall was fading into the background. I tried to picture my Mary and my daughters, but I could not.

"Why did my passing have to hurt so bad?" I whispered, more to myself than audibly.

"Because of His suffering on the cross for your salvation. It is the price one must pay. The pain was the shedding of sin." The voice had a musical quality to it now. It seemed more like singing in my head then actual spoken words. "For all have sinned and come short of His Glory."

I began to sing to myself as I flew along, while being cradled in the one very strong arm of this Being. I began to feel a powerful affection for her or it, as we moved through space—or, at least I think so. It was not dark and yet there was no light either. It just *was*—and that's the only way I can explain it. I wish I could tell you I arrived in heaven and saw Jesus and Mommy and Daddy dancing by the Jordan River, but this is where the dream ended.

I woke up in my bunk in our private Oak Ridge Boys bus somewhere in Iowa by a Hampton Inn—and that was it. I got up, poured some coffee, gathered my bags, and walked unsteadily to my hotel room. I sat in a chair for a long time and pondered this vision over and over in my mind.

My brain reeled with memories of family, bowling, Taylor Swift, a goofy red sweater, death and decay, and a conversation with a heavenly Being. What did it all mean? I really don't know.

There are lots of things we don't know about. But my Bible tells me the secret things are known only to God, so I may have to wait for parts of this dream to be revealed to me when the former things all pass away, and everything becomes new as I take that last journey through space and time into eternity . . . Perhaps in the arms of an angel.

A humorous addendum: I once dreamed of the college football playoffs. In my dream Alabama would play Oklahoma and Michigan State would play comic Larry the Cable Guy. MSU was picked to win by 56 points. I took Larry and the points. When I told Larry about it, he said, "You should find it very disturbing that I am even IN your dreams." HAHA!

One more: There is a Johnny Cash poem called "The Spirit Rider" which was put to music a few years ago by singer-songwriter Jamey Johnson. I just love the idea of the ghostly rider riding on and on and on.

One night recently I dreamed I saw him. He rode a huge gray horse and wore a long gray duster and a gray cowboy hat. As he galloped through the snow (I think), I began to see him up close. He had on a black shirt under his duster with the collar pulled up high around his profile so I couldn't quite make out his face. As dreams will do, I was able to pan closer. I could now hear and feel the beating hooves and smell the leather of the tack when, at last, he turned and looked my way. I saw his full face! The Spirit Rider . . . was me!

He/I smiled, and I woke up . . . 🖊

CHAPTER 75

Play a good song.

I see myself loving music for as long as I can remember. In fact, the music business has been the focal point of my entire adult life. That would be performance, recording, management, production, logistics, marketing, promotion, touring, and publishing—and even a bit of songwriting from time to time.

I have spent my years surrounded by singers and musicians and songwriters, most of whom possessed more talent than me. And I have been blessed with the fact that I am always learning from them. As a singer, I have known the best! Singing next to Duane Allen on stage for over fifty years has been more of a constant study in how to sing than anything I could have ever learned in any other forum.

As a banjo student, I have had the opportunity to study many great players and see how they apply and hone their craft over time. I am thankful for the opportunity to glean and share in that knowledge. The Mighty Oaks Band is the most respected group of players in the business. They are all great guys and, man, they can play! I have learned much from each of them.

Living in Nashville, one comes in constant contact with the finest songwriters in the world. It is impossible not to pick up a hint or two or three on how to construct a song. The plain and simple truth: I sing songs for a living, and it has been a wondrous and incredible journey to be sure. I thank God for this career every single day.

As a fan, my taste in music is very eclectic. My music library is full of variety, and the genres of the stuff I listen to stretch and blur the lines between rock and country and bluegrass and classical. I am not sure how to categorize Frank Sinatra, Dean Martin, and Johnny Mathis, but I assure you they are there.

I never have liked labels though. To me, music is good, or it is not good. You either like it, or you do not. The bottom line is the song—and I am about to elaborate. Whether I am listening to Bruce Springsteen, Andrea Bocelli, Billy Strings, or the Gaither Vocal Band, I am always looking for the great song. Carrie Underwood singing "Jesus, Take the Wheel," Brad Paisley and Dolly Parton singing "When I Get Where I Am Going," Brooks & Dunn singing "Believe," Vince Gill singing "Go Rest High on That Mountain," Janet Paschal singing "Another Soldier's Coming Home," or Bob Seger singing, well, almost anything. But you get the picture.

As the longtime lead voice of the Oak Ridge Boys, Duane Allen would say, "It is the song that matters."

He calls it three minutes of magic and, thankfully, we have had our share of great songs to sing over all these years.

Sometimes I will scan across the radio dial, saying, "Come on, someone play me a great song! Please!"

Sometimes one will wade through a ton of mediocrity before landing on that piece of magic. Whether it is a big hit or a demo by an obscure writer or perhaps a deep album cut that jumps out and grabs you right by the heart, it is the song! It is the song!

I am fond of saying all music was once new, and that is a truism. Duane would answer it is only the great songs that stand the test of time, and we are both correct in the analysis.

Every song was indeed once new but not necessarily worth keeping on the playlist. Can you say "My Way" by the Chairman, or "The Pretender" by Jackson Browne? How about "In Color" by Jamey Johnson, or "Come Jesus Come" by Stephen McWhirter? I do not know much about the urban hip-hop kind of music that is played today, except to say it is perhaps the only genre I find distasteful—and not because I am a white boy. I just cannot find "the song" in there. It is all beat and rhythmic poetry of sorts which does not apply to my life, so I guess I block it out. I do, however, love rhythm and blues.

Give me Gladys Knight or the Stylistics any day to Lil Wayne or Eminem. Remember "Midnight Train to Georgia"? *Woo Woo!* It is, perhaps, relevant that I never cared much for disco music either, but I have always loved the Bee Gees. The vocal thing and the incomparable songwriting are probably the reason. They have recorded many great songs, before and after disco, when they were "Jive Talkin'" us to death. I also love that "Old Time Rock and Roll"—that sort of music just makes me smile.

I have written much about Elvis, but I also loved many of the other early acts of that day—for example, Ricky Nelson, "Hello Mary Lou, Goodbye Heart." The doo-wop groups of the late fifties and early sixties are also very meaningful. Danny & the Juniors' "At the Hop" still works for me. The big admission: I did not like the British Invasion of 1964. I did not even like the Beatles, although my respect for them has grown over time. I just thought acts like the Dave Clark Five, Herman's Hermits, and the Rolling Stones were ushering in a big change, and I was not happy with it.

Hey, I was in high school. I was chasing girls. I was trying to find myself. I thought it was the end of my kind of rock and roll—and you know what? It was!

The British groups set the table for the late sixties, free love, and hippie flower power, protest songs, much of which had an almost evil edge. The war in Vietnam, the ugly race riots, assassinations, and the drug culture had a lot to do with that, of course. But, eventually the soft rock of the Eagles, Jackson Browne, and Fleetwood Mac would rescue us all from "The Eve of Destruction."

But for me? I turned my attention to gospel quartets and Merle Haggard, and I am happy to say I still listen to them today. My favorite gospel groups have changed a bit from the old Statesmen, Blackwood Brothers, and Cathedral Quartet to Ernie Haas and Signature Sound, the Gaithers, and the Isaacs. And as far as traditional country is concerned, I am happy I managed to cross paths with the likes of Merle Haggard, George Jones, Charlie Pride, and so many other legends.

As a banjo player, I listen to a ton of bluegrass music, and I love all the major acts because they can really pick. As they say, a bad musician cannot hide in top-tier bluegrass. If I grabbed my banjo and sat in with Dailey & Vincent or Ricky Skaggs and Kentucky Thunder, someone just might open fire. But as a professional singer, I constantly find myself navigating from gospel to country, while I still possess an old rocker's heart and energy and attitude.

I guess I have made a pretty good living by riding upon that rail for a long time now. It is this kind of open-mindedness and being willing to stretch the musical boundaries that has kept the Oak Ridge Boys alive for decades. Four different men with four different backgrounds stand on a stage every night and make magic happen, and it is a joyful thing to be a part of. I learn something from my singing partners, Duane Allen, William Lee Golden, and Richard Sterban, every single day.

There is a right way and there is a "no way." I thank God daily for placing me with a group of men who are always forward thinking, yet possess a firm hold on the traditions of who and what we are. We are not the young guys anymore, but we are still out here singing to a lot of people year after year.

We are so very thankful to God above for the good health and for the ability to still be grinding it out on the never-ending tour. We give Him the honor, praise, and glory for these blessings. I have never taken the music for granted. To me it is a daily gift, and I do not believe I could ever exist without it.

A great producer once told me if you take care of the music, then the music will take care of you. I have done my best to take care of the music. But I could never give back enough to make up for the constant joy that it has given to *me* over my entire life.

Somebody, please play a good song!

CHAPTER 76

Let's sing!

I see myself and my singing partners emerging from the Covid pandemic a few years back. I promised in the front of this book I would not address the dark days of the pandemic and shutdowns, and I don't plan to write much about it now either, except to say it sure felt good to get back to singing.

The Oak Ridge Boys started to see mask-less, sold-out crowds enjoying concerts again. You could once again see their smiles and observe that spark in their eyes. I remember so-called experts saying even when all of this was over people will never shake hands or hug strangers ever again—nothing could have been further from the truth. People were so happy to be back to normal; they were all hugging and shaking hands even more than before!

Thankfully things seem much brighter now than back in 2020, when people were told to stay home, while wiping their behinds with a coffee filter and trying not to die. It was indeed a tough time for everyone. However good things kept happening to the Oak Ridge Boys.

In August of 2020 we recorded a new album that brought us a certain amount of accomplishment and purpose—we just may have recorded the perfect album for the times. Old gospel songs and new gospel songs, as well as classic country songs, and some terrific new songs as well, written just for us by some of the best songwriters in Nashville.

Our young and accomplished producer Dave Cobb led the way creatively and the result was *Front Porch Singin'* which released in June of 2021, thanks, also, to the young and forward-thinking head of Lightning Rod Records, Logan Rogers. Check it out. There are blessings and a good dose of ORB magic on these tracks.

Yes, our mantra has always been "Let's Sing!" In good times or sad times, we just keep on singing our songs, and God has always blessed our efforts. Life can be uncertain sometimes, but the good news for the believer is that Jesus Christ is NOT uncertain. He is the same yesterday, today and forever, and He loves us dearly.

Though I have experienced uncertainty in my life from time to time, my faith in Jesus never let me worry about things or lose hope. We have a song that we have been singing for several years that says, "There Will be Light."

Jesus IS the Light and the Bible tells us that in Him there is no darkness at all (1 John 1:5). I believe this to be true! So let's sing! 🎤

CHAPTER 77

What will heaven be like?

I see myself musing about heaven. There is a wonderful Oak Ridge Boys song called "Before I Die" that William Lee Golden interprets beautifully on the lead vocal. Fans always referred to it as a "bucket list" song.

Now I am not sure if the bucket list idea started with the Jack Nicholson/Morgan Freeman movie or if it existed long before that, but it sure has had an effect on society. People are always coming up with a special list of things they would like to do before passing on—from writing that novel to hang gliding through the Alps, or having a cup of tea while watching the sun rise over the Serengeti in the company of a pride of lions.

I wonder if a bucket list is so popular because many folks are unhappy with the life they lead, or if it is just the adventurous part of us that rises inside. Hey, it is awesome to have a goal and a dream and then work to that end. But I confess I have no bucket list. It just doesn't interest me. Perhaps it is because so many of my dreams have already been realized or, perhaps, I am just feeling very blessed and happy in my own skin. But I think the big reason I feel no real need for an exotic adventure before my death is because Jesus Christ is first and foremost in my heart and life—what lies before me is much more exciting than snowboarding through the Himalayas.

196

It is heaven that matters most as our life winds down. Our times are but a vapor passing quickly, and our vapors seem to be moving right on along. I have spoken with many older citizens over the years and each one, without fail, say they marveled at how fast the sand fell to the bottom of their hourglass.

We never would have believed that in our younger days, when a simple day at school seemed to last a week. As we get older, I assure you, faithful reader, the world does seem to spin faster upon its axis, and I am good with that.

It feels like just the other day I was that young Philly kid who dreamed of singing songs. I seemingly woke up just a few hours later, and I was in my seventies. The Bible teaches us quite plainly that it is appointed unto man and every other living creature once to die, so we are all going (Hebrews 9:27).

What most of us don't know is the time or the place or how it all might end. I have made it a lot farther down the road than many of my dear friends. I know from experience that, although Jesus has prepared a wondrous place for us, nobody has a burning desire to hasten the journey.

The ability to breathe air and live on this earth is one of God's greatest gifts. I have seen friends, loved ones, and even animals, fight with every fiber of their being to stay alive. Death is not very pretty sometimes, but the journey beyond is full of mystery and wonderment.

So just what is over there? What will heaven be like? Unlike the unbeliever, I do believe in heaven. I cannot imagine when a soul leaves this empty shell of a body behind that it wanders off into some eternal darkness or, worse yet, comes back as a frog.

With a little bit of faith and knowledge of the Bible, the hereafter that Jesus speaks about is a lot easier to believe. One day we shall pass out of this life and into the next. The shell of every living thing at one point or another will eventually go back to being part of the earth. Ashes to ashes, dust to dust.

Death is an end, yet it is a wondrous beginning for those of us who believe in Jesus Christ as a personal Savior. But what happens after we cross that old, chilly Jordan is as much of a mystery now as it has ever been. Oh, lots of people have written about near-death experiences, where they saw the Light or God or other glorious sights, and many of these experiences possess a ring of truth—especially the accounts of little children like the boy in the book *Heaven Is Real* or the girl in *Miracles from Heaven*.

It does seem that little children are seeing things we cannot see. My wife calls it angels in the architecture, and she is not off the track here.

We are continuously under siege by the minions of hell, and there is a constant battle going on between these powers of darkness and God's holy angels of Light that is mercifully shielded from our finite vision because we probably could not handle such a sight.

Someday when all things are revealed, and we exist on a much higher plane, we will understand. But for now, we are seeing through a glass darkly and this is not a bad thing.

Perhaps God does reveal a vision or two to children from time to time. How many times have you seen a baby stare wide-eyed with pure wonder at something that seems to be way beyond anything you can see or even imagine? Angels? Perhaps.

Jesus said, "Let the little children come to me, and do not hinder them, for the kingdom of heaven belongs to such as these" (Matthew 19:14).

He also spoke of a childlike faith to open our hearts and minds to all that is possible through Him. Unless we become as little children, we will never enter the kingdom of heaven."

Which brings me back to my original question: Just what is over there?

Lazarus came forth from the dead at Christ's command, but I do not remember reading very much about his experience. *Where did you go, Laz? What was it like? Were there bright lights? Musical flowers?* Never addressed.

Jesus took the time to give us a bit of a look at the hereafter when He said, "I go to prepare a place for you that, where I am, there you will be as well. In my Father's house are many mansions; if it were not so, I would have told you" (paraphrase of John 14:2–3)

I go to prepare a place for you so that where I am, you will be also. What a promise from Jesus Himself.

He who has ears . . . let him hear . . . and believe! There are many songs and hymns of the gospel that contain a plethora of verses regarding promised streets of purest gold and walls of jasper and gates of pearl, yet these could all be just metaphors for something so glorious that our human mind could never fathom it.

If mansions or crowns or perhaps a jeweled walkway were what we desired, I might suggest that would be a bit shallow. Heaven will be much more—and I sincerely believe precious saints of God are looking forward to other aspects with more anticipation. Although, I'll bet that my Mary will be looking forward to every jewel she can lay her hands on. (Just kidding, honey!)

Will we know each other in heaven? You bet! We will be known as we are known! This is my favorite promise (1 Corinthians 13:12). When I see those friends and loved ones who have gone on before, residing in perfect and healthy new spiritual bodies, I think in one glance I will see them at every age.

I will see a young version of my mother, while at the same time seeing her in a later time, and she will be so very happy. She will know me as well in the same way, and she will hold me for as long as she cares to hold her son because passing time will not be an issue in eternity.

There will be great rejoicing and homecomings and tears of joy and happiness. Yes, this sounds like the heaven that God speaks of when He says that no good thing will be withheld from us (Psalm 84:11).

Perhaps it will be multi-dimensional, where layer after layer of places exist. Maybe just by thinking or wishing for something, it will happen. *I want to see Jesus* . . . there He is. *I want to chat with Abraham Lincoln* . . . it happens. *I want to laugh with my daddy* . . . it happens. *I want to see my Mary* . . . There she is. Just like that!

I like to believe there will be animals there. Lions will not only lie down with lambs, but precious pets who meant so much to us on earth may appear at the mention of their name or the celestial thought of the memory of them. *Where is my Barney cat?* There he is! *Where is my little Omaha kitty?* He is right there! *Hello, Molly! Hello, Sally Ann!*

There will be light and flowers and music the likes of which our human form cannot imagine. Angels and saints singing praise to the King! Choirs and instruments galore, and I plan on singing right along with all my gospel music friends who have gone before.

Jesus Himself will be on every level of this wonderful place. He will shine a perfect Light upon all of us who have accepted Him as Lord and Savior and King of our lives. And His constant love will burn and shimmer within our spirits. The feeling will be one of pure joy on a level unimagined.

This is obviously all conjecture and happy musings, of course. What may come to be and what may not come to be are truly not known by any of us. But it is fun to think about, and it is a blessing and a comfort to know that farther along we will know all about it!

Farther along all our questions will have answers, as is His promise. I am standing on these promises of Christ, our Lord.

In the meantime, we live our lives here and live them more abundantly, thanks to our faith in Christ. This life below is a wonderful journey, and I am thankful for every single day and every single memory. I am thankful for my family, my friends, and for my crossroads. And I am thankful for songs that are sung and words that are written.

One day we will sit in Glory and, perhaps, reflect upon these short days before eternity. Or perhaps not. But I do know this much: we will be healthy and strong, and we will be surrounded by friends and loved ones, and God's Holy Ones will minister to our very souls.

To quote the great gospel songwriter Jim Hill, "What a day that will be!"

I will also quote a song I wrote several years back called "The Journey":

Oh brother, my dear brother
Your life could end today
Except a man be born again
He cannot see the way
For Jesus there is waiting
To lead us past the grave
And take us home to be with Him
When the final journey's made.

So I guess the point of all this is that what happens before we die is not nearly as important or rewarding as what comes after. However, as we pass through this life, we should strive to be a positive force for good and for God every single day, because only what is done for Christ will truly last!

CHAPTER 78

End of Days?

I see myself these days living somewhat in a bubble, and I am very happy with my life exactly as it is. At seventy-six years of age, I feel as though I have earned my bubble. I didn't say my head was in the sand—I just do not concern myself as much these days with the goings-on of the universe. In other words, the older I have become the larger my "I don't give a rip list" has become.

But world issues are hard to totally ignore.

Over the last several years there has been unusual violence in the streets of our American cities, universities, and around the world. Russia has invaded Ukraine. Hamas has invaded Israel in one of the most hideous displays of barbarism since the Holocaust. China is looking at overtaking Taiwan, and Iranian backed forces are lobbing missiles at American military bases, while all kinds of people are crossing our borders by the millions illegally.

We may be in the middle or the end of World War III, or perhaps another 9/11 type event, by the time you hold this book in your hands. The devil seems to be running loose all over the world right now, and it makes me wonder if we are approaching the End of Days and the return of our Messiah.

As we wait, though, we need to pray unceasingly for America and the world and remember to keep our own head on a swivel and be cognizant of the evil around us. I promised myself this would not be a political book, so I will go no further here except to ask God to please bless us all!

CHAPTER 79

Another pathway with a new horizon . . . I'm good with it as everything ends with Jesus.

I see myself writing a final chapter and, perhaps, my final chapter ever. As I finish this book, it is now early in 2024. I can't believe I have been working on this project since 2021.

If you have stayed with me through the musings and memories, you know I mentioned in chapter 65 about my crippling leg issues, and it would now seem, according to Mayo Clinic and Vanderbilt neurology, that I have been dealing with a slow onset of Amyotrophic Lateral Sclerosis.

As I write, very few people outside of my family know about this because I didn't want people feeling sorry for me. But, by the time this book is published, hopefully sometime this year, I would imagine it will be common knowledge.

I am not sure how the rest of my life might play out right now but, believe me, I am not down about it. I made it to seventy-one years old without any health issues. I could run through a wall. But, these days, it's all about walkers and stair lifts and wheelchairs and a lot of help from friends and family—and especially my wonderful wife.

If you have been to a show over those past days, you will have seen that I was still singing right on through the Christmas tour of 2023. The guys helped me onstage, and I would blast away from a stool. But by the last show, I knew I was through! I couldn't even climb aboard the tour bus.

I announced my retirement and just mentioned a neuro-muscular disorder as the reason. The Oak Ridge Boys announced the "American Made Farewell Tour" for 2024 with plans to record a new album, but I will not be taking part. A young protégé named Ben James will be singing in my place, and he will do a great job.

Folks watching me through 2023 could easily tell my physical body was struggling, although my voice and my sheer will did remain strong through it all. ALS is a life-changing neuro-muscular disease where your brain ceases to send neurons to the nerves that control your muscles, forcing them to weaken and eventually to atrophy and paralysis.

The experts say every case is different and there is some great research going on right now, which is hopeful. I feel blessed that the onset, which began with a weakness in my left leg and foot, has lasted over four years now.

As I finish this book, both legs are gone, and my hands are leaving me. I am typing with just four fingers but thus far, I can swallow, talk, and even sing a bit and my breathing has only been affected by about 20 percent according to my latest test.

Friends, I believe in my heart that God has me in the palm of His mighty hand, so I am not fearful. To me, I just see myself traversing another pathway with a new horizon and, again, I am good with it as everything ends with Jesus.

So the guy who used to sing and run around the stage, play sports, pick banjo, cut big fields, and possess a boundless energy can't take a step without help these days. But I feel so blessed that it waited until my seventies to appear. Many are not as fortunate. I still believe my Jesus can heal me if it be His will but if not, I have lived a life like few have—a Philly kid who became a fifty-year member of the legendary Oak Ridge Boys.

I am fortunate and blessed to have had a ton of love and support from my family and my friends, and I truly believe that LOVE is all that matters along our journey. For love is all we take with us when we leave this earth.

Perhaps this is the reason this verse of Scripture has become so meaningful to me over the last few years:

"Two are better than one, because they have a good return for their labor: If either of them falls down, one can help the other up. But pity anyone who falls and has no one to help them up." (Ecclesiastes 4:9–10)

I am thankful that I am NOT alone. I am constantly lifted up and constantly loved. So please don't feel sorry for me. I will do my best to fight this thing and keep my eyes on Jesus. And, when it is time to shed this human form and fly away, I will be moving to that final Home where I will again be able to run through green pastures and sing songs, hang with my parents, and wait for my Mary. It will be wonderful.

I may be gone when you read this book and, if so, it is my prayer you will have found encouragement in my little memoirs and stories—and hopefully the Light of the gospel will have shone through.

Selah.
Thanks for reading! JSB 🎤

"The smallest feline is a masterpiece."
—Leonardo da Vinci

~

In his hand is the life of every creature
and the breath of all mankind.
—Job 12:10

~

Cats come into your home to teach you about affection;
they leave to teach you about loss.
—Jules Verne

Bonus Reading
The Story of Sally Ann

After our dear Sally Ann kitty passed in May of 2020 at twenty-two years old, I wrote the following story. My friend and best-selling author Andy Andrews read it and advised me NOT to let a publisher just turn it into an illustrated children's book, and that is what started to happen.

This is not a children's book, although I would love for children to enjoy it. This is a story for cat lovers and Oak Ridge Boys fans, and I am honored to include it in this book.

Thank you for reading about our Sally Ann. JSB

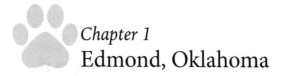

Chapter 1
Edmond, Oklahoma

The Oklahoma City businessman loved his home in the town of Edmond, and he didn't even mind the commute to his office each day. He would put on his suit and tie, jump into his jacked-up Ford F-150 truck, turn up the sound of his favorite radio station, and rock it all the way to OKC and back again. Since his wife passed away a few years ago, and with no children, it seemed his entire life centered around his job, and he was good at it. There wasn't a problem he couldn't solve or an issue he could not fix, and the thought made him smile.

The back porch of his home backed up to a cornfield, a tree line, and several acres of wooded area. Each evening, he would come home from work, shower, put on comfy clothes, and sit on his back porch with his feet propped up on the cross beam, and gaze out at God's beauty while allowing his mind to wander. He made a good living, for which he was very grateful, and he was quite content and about as happy as a man alone could possibly be.

As a Christian, he knew God had blessed him way beyond deserving and he had a peaceful assurance that his sweet wife was looking over him and one day he would see her again as was His promise. He came out to this deck every single night, no matter the weather and prayed and thought about her.

He had just taken his seat on the beautifully designed porch with the cool deck he had built for himself when he saw the cat . . . again. He had seen her several times over the last several months, thinking she might be living under the house but wasn't sure. He left food and water out for her on several occasions, but she never touched any of it. She was a wild one for sure. She never came close to the house but remained aloof and guarded. The man felt sorry for the feral kitty because, like him, she seemed quite alone in the world.

That would be the last time he would ever see the cat.

A few weeks later on a warm August morning, when he decided to have his morning coffee and fried egg sandwich on the back porch, he heard a sound.

Ewe.

What was that?

Ewe . . .

There it was again, but a bit louder this time. He walked down the two steps leading from the deck to the stretch of lawn between his house and the woods.

EWE!

He suddenly realized the sound was actually coming from beneath the porch, so he knelt down and cautiously peered into the semi-darkness, half expecting a wildcat or a raccoon might attack and then claw his eyes out.

He detected a slight movement about three feet from where he was kneeling. *Yep, something is in there,* but he couldn't tell what.

He ran inside and snatched a tactical flashlight from his drawer by the bed. Turning on the light to half brightness, he saw the kitten. One very small kitty with its blue eyes barely open.

"Are you all alone, little fella?" He gently drew the kitten from beneath the porch. It fit in the palm of his hand, and he was at a total loss of what to do for this poor little creature.

After looking everywhere for a sign of the mother cat or any more babies, he took the kitten into the house and wrapped it in a towel before he thumbed through the Yellow Pages.

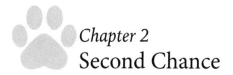

Chapter 2
Second Chance

The businessman fingered his way through the list of animal shelters in the phone book, while petting the little kitten all the while.

There it is, he thought.

He called the Second Chance Animal Shelter in Norman, which was about forty miles down the road.

A welcoming voice answered. "Second Chance, how can I help you?"

After the man told his story and answered a few questions, the kind lady asked him to bring the kitten to Norman as soon as possible, and that is just what the Oklahoma City businessman did. He knew that, with his schedule, there was no way he could ever care for it, and there was no sign of the mother cat who had birthed just one little brown-and-black-striped kitten.

So the abandoned kitten was now in the care of the fine folks at Second Chance, and they nursed it and cared for it and named it Armond.

It soon came to pass that the Oak Ridge Boys were playing the state fair in OKC, and your author had just released a children's book series based on his own cats. The first two books in what would become a series of four, *Molly* and *The Home* had just been released by Ideals children's books, and on this show day I was to appear at a Walden's bookstore in a local mall. As was the case many times at such events, we asked a local animal shelter to join us, so I not only signed and sold a few books, but the local shelter promoted responsible pet ownership and even helped a few cats find a forever home.

Before the folks lined up, I was enjoying looking at the kitties that Second Chance had brought to the event from Norman, when all of a sudden, my heart stopped as I beheld the cutest little kitten I had ever seen. The nice lady let me pick him up and hold him. I didn't want to let go, so I set him on my shoulder and there he stayed for the entire event.

The Oak Ridge Boys fans and book fans lined up for almost two hours, and everyone who walked by me was taken with my kitten. Second Chance Animal Shelter found homes for quite a few cats that day.

I called my wife who was known as Mother Mary in the Molly the Cat book series, a human-cat mother who loved ALL kitties. And even though her hands were full with the four cats we already had, I tried to talk her into a fifth one.

Mary didn't like the fact that it was a boy. She said she would rather have a little girl if she was adding a new family member, but she eventually said yes. I was so excited that I named the kitten Boomer Sooner and made plans to take him with me. But Second Chance said no. The kitty was not quite old enough, so I would have to wait at least a week.

Well, next week I was coming back to Oklahoma with the Boys to play the Tulsa fair, and I thought that maybe we could work something out. The Second Chance ladies said they would gladly bring the kitten to Tulsa.

Two wonderful ladies drove over 120 miles to bring me that little kitten.

Chapter 3
Bus Ride

Well, right before our big show, the kitten arrived. I had security guards looking out for the Second Chance ladies and Boomer. I was beside myself when they arrived. I had prepared the back lounge of the Oak Ridge Boys tour bus with a small litter box, bowls, a few toys, kitten food, and a little bed I had made from cardboard and a towel. After the ladies left to drive back to Oklahoma City, I introduced Boomer to all the guys and then put the kitten in the back room, while we sang for the fine folks at the fair that night.

After the show I ran to the back of the bus to check on him, and he seemed just fine. He had eaten a bit and even used the litter box. Our tour bus took off for home, while our band was still playing us off stage.

It was so much fun messing with a kitten on the bus ride home. I stayed up with him long after the other Oaks had crawled into their sleeping bunks. The kitten fell asleep, so I decided to put him in my bunk with me for the 10-hour trip home to Hendersonville, Tennessee. I placed him on the inside of my rolling bed, right by my head, and there he stayed all night long either content or petrified at the whole ordeal—it was hard to tell. I called Mary and caught her up and she said I should take the kitten by our vet before I brought him home. After we rolled in, I did just that.

After Boomer Sooner was given a clean bill of health and a shot, the doc revealed to me that Boomer was NOT a him at all but a little girl. The lady at the desk started a file on Boomer, and I told her to hold off on the name. *Just wait until Mary finds out she is a little GIRL kitty! She will want to name her.* I was sure that Armond or Boomer Sooner was NOT going to wash.

Chapter 4
Sally Ann

We already had four cats I kind of made famous in my Molly the Cat book series. There was Old Pumpkin, who I made into a wise old sage and our little Omaha kitty (yes, we found him in Omaha), who was Molly's best friend Omi. And Gypsy Lee, our big girl, who was the self-appointed guardian of The Home. And, of course, Molly herself . . . our star whose wonderful adventures were loved by children everywhere in those days!

When Mary first laid eyes on the new little brown-and-black now-female tiger kitty from Oklahoma, she cried with joy. It was love at first sight on both sides. It was as if they both knew they would be best friends for a long time. Every cat makes their own place in this world, not really influenced much by other cats or even humans. They just follow their own heart and trust their soul. Therefore, cats are so very unique, and we just knew this new kitten was beyond special.

For several weeks we kept the kitten in a spare bedroom by herself so she could adjust to her surroundings, which of course included four other curious cats on the other side of the door. She was not alone often, for Mary was with her almost all the time, talking to her, playing with her, and feeding her. One day I looked in on Mary as she was loving on the kitten.

She looked up at me with tears in her eyes and softly said, "I am going to name her Sally Ann . . . my precious little Sally."

There was no way Mary could have known that the two ladies from the Second Chance Animal Shelter in Norman, Oklahoma, who brought her to me in Tulsa were BOTH named . . . SALLY!

Chapter 5

Sally Ann never got very big. She was just a little cat, but she had a tough feral side, and from early on she let the other cats know big-time that, although she may be little, she be FIERCE! In fact, that sign hangs on the wall above one of her beds and, to be honest, no other cat ever gave her too hard of a time. As the new Queen of the house, Sally Ann could always do anything she wanted to do and go anywhere she wanted to go. She slept anywhere she wanted to sleep, and Mary always made sure she had her favorite foods in her bowl. Yes, we have always referred to her as our Queen, but as you know cats always seem to gain multiple names. Sometimes we called her a little duck or teapot, or Dart because she was fast. I usually called her Little Sals. But mostly we referred to her as our Sally Ann.

Sally Ann lived through several sets of cats, and we always joked she didn't really like any of them. But she did love several very much. As far as humans were concerned, she pretty much endured me and the daughters and grandkids over the years, but the love that she and Mary shared together was something to behold.

Now, we are cat people and we have always had a houseful of them and, as stated earlier, they are all different. And they all fill their own space pretty much like we all do. They are all so very special, and we love each one. But that bond between Mary and Sally was just so very special. They were two peas in a pod, and I swear they communicated with each other on an amazing level. I believe if Mary were to say, "Hey Sally, go make me some iced tea," Sally would have understood every single word. Of course, she would not be brewing any tea for Mary because, after all, she was still a cat—even if she COULD have, she probably still would have NOT! However, I have seen Mary feed her certain foods because as she would say, "That's what Sally asked for!" I have never seen such a thing in my entire life and perhaps I never will again. This friendship lasted just over twenty-two years.

To a cat lover, their own cat is the best one ever, and I am certain that it is true. We have shared our lives and our home with many great cats, and we have always been the better for the experience. If I might paraphrase Mark Twain, "A home without a cat—and a well-fed, well-petted and properly revered cat—may be a perfect home, perhaps, but how can it prove its worth?" I concur with Mr. Clemens.

Year after year, Sally was loved and looked after, and she gave so much back in return. Her presence in our home was a constant adventure in life and love. There was no way one could NOT have loved this little girl kitty. She was a light, and I am certain God had His hand upon her from the very start.

Sally Ann left us the other day at the ripe old age of twenty-two. Yes, it seemed like time was against her as it most certainly is against us all.

As a side note, back in the Molly book days, we had a website online complete with a message board where children and adults could communicate with your author or Mother Mary or Molly. We would pretend that Sally Ann hosted the forum and she complained often about being the only cat in The Home who was not included in a book. We would say that

Sally was miffed. It was fun, and we have laughed about it for years. Well, I am not sure this piece will become a book, but I AM writing about her.

Mother Mary's cat hospice was in full mode looking after Sally Ann until the end. She seemed pretty much herself right up until a month before she passed. But, alas, she slid downhill very quickly.

Near the end Mary would take her outside and let her smell the fresh air, while always reminding her about her beginnings in Oklahoma, about the nice businessman and Second Chance, and Sally and Sally, and how I brought her home aboard a show bus. And then Mary would remind her how much she was loved. I am so happy I was here to see it.

One afternoon Sally was in her bed, and Mary was right beside her. Sally shuddered a bit, and Mary spoke to her softly.

"This will be the hardest thing you ever have to do!" Mary whispered.

The last thing Mary ever said to her was "Jesus loves you. Sally Ann. He really, really does."

And with Mary's hand upon her, Sally Ann passed on quietly and sweetly to that Better Place that God has prepared for creatures such as her.

Goodbye, Little Sals . . . We WILL see you again. Our home will never be the same without you.

Addendum

Mary wrapped her gently in a small case complete with toys and a time capsule and a blue bow in order to prepare her for her final resting place here in our cat cemetery, which lies down a hill under a huge tree. So many of our past kitties rest here, and it's comforting to know that Molly, Omaha, Pumpkin, and so many others are resting right there with her.

While Mary was preparing her, I solemnly dug a grave just up from the others as Mary wanted Sally Ann to be closer to the house. Then the strangest thing happened. I saw several deer heading toward me, which is no surprise as we have deer around much of the time. But then here came a few more and then several more after that. Altogether, about fifteen deer gathered, looked our way, and then kneeled down at once. I kid you not. I have the photos. Now I am not trying to say that the deer knew . . . But maybe they did.

Animals sense things on a different plane than do humans, and perhaps they were paying a special tribute to a special little life force who was on her way home. It was seriously angelic in nature, and I am not exaggerating. I sat down and cried for a long time after that. My soul seemed comforted. To me it was God reaffirming, as only He can, that everything matters. The smallest of creatures matter . . . Therefore, I matter, and YOU matter.

Perhaps it was a final thank-you from Sally Ann as well . . . for a life well lived . . . and for the LOVE!

As a final side note, Mary and I started a foundation years ago when I wrote the Molly the Cat book series, whose mission is to assist in children's literacy and to provide funds for various cat-related care services, including no-kill rescue shelters all over America. We are self-funded for the most part, but as a 501c entity we welcome tax-free donations. We made a generous donation to Second Chance Animal Shelter in Oklahoma City in the name of our Sally Ann.

The Joseph S. and Mary Ann Bonsall Foundation
16845 Kercheval, Suite 5,
Grosse Pointe, MI 48230

The Thank-Yous

Thank you, Gary Terashita and Fidelis Publishing, for your input, your vision, and for giving this book a chance. I am honored to be part of this great group of authors at Fidelis.

Thank you, longtime friend, associate, fellow author, and agent Kathy Harris for once again finding the right home for a Bonsall book. You are the best!

Thank you, Dr. Megan Settle, Dr. Robert Pilkington, Dr. Marc Tressler, Dr. Cliff Brown, Dr. William Liggett, Dr. Warren Rose, Dr. Dwaine Allison, Dr. Mike Ritchie, Dr. Sarah Berini, and Mayo Clinic Neurology, and my current care team at Vanderbilt Neurology led by Dr. Amanda Peltier and Dr. Sara Martin. Each one has contributed mightily to my journey. Many thanks also to Amedysis Pallative Care and Alive Hospice.

I am forever grateful to Laura Welch and New Leaf Press for publishing *G.I. Joe and Lillie.*

To my partners Duane Allen, William Lee Golden, and Richard Sterban: together for decades, our brotherhood, friendship, and harmony took us way beyond our dreams.

A special thank you to Duane Allen and Darrick Kinslow for getting me through the tour after my legs stopped working, and also to Duane Allen, your precious words that you were kind enough to write in the Foreword made me weep like a little boy! You have been my mentor, my hero, my friend, and my brother for sixty years. I love you too, Mighty Ace!

Thank you to longtime friend and attorney S. Gary Spicer for your constant guidance and counsel.

To my family: Daughters, Jennifer and Sabrina; Doug and Danny; grandkids, Luke and Breanne; great-grandsons, Chance and Grey; my sister, Nancy, and Chuck; and especially my precious Mary, who is not only the love of my life but has been amazing doing things that nobody sees . . . I so adore her.

Thank you to Jon Mir, Ginger Key, Jim Halsey, Mike Pitcock, and Doug Brant. Each one has stepped up for me.

To Norah Lee Allen, who left this earth for Heaven last spring, for her love and never-ending friendship all these years. Heaven's gain . . . It seems so many are leaving right now. To Rusty Golden, who passed shortly before this book went to print. See you there, brother!

Thank you to the Father, the Son, and the Holy Spirit for blessing my life way beyond any deserving on my part and for the promise of healing and heaven. I love You, Jesus!

A final blurb about the blurbers who took the time to read an early manuscript and then write a blurb about it. (This line should drive an editor insane.)

Scott McKain A dear friend for decades, Scott has become the most sought-after public speaker and author in the country. He teaches major corporations how to improve their business and how to treat people right!

Jimmy Wayne Not only a great singer and hitmaker, but as a child, Jimmy fell through the cracks of the foster system and a few years ago wrote a book about it called *Walk to Beautiful*, which is one of the finest books I have ever read.

Bill Gaither Bill and his lovely wife, Gloria, have written some of the finest gospel songs ever. The Gaither Homecoming video series has breathed incredible life into the southern gospel music industry. I first saw Bill singing when I was in high school with his Gaither Trio consisting of his brother, Danny, his wife, Gloria, and Bill himself on piano. I never dreamed we would become so close over all these years.

Joe West He has umpired more major league games than any other umpire in history, and we were honored to be at his record-setting game in Chicago a few years back. He is known in baseball circles as Country Joe West because of his love of country music. He has been a great friend of the Oak Ridge Boys and a great personal friend to me over all these years! YER OUT!!

Zach Williams When I first heard Zach sing "Chain Breaker," I became an immediate fan of his stellar songwriting and incredible voice. His talents have led many to Christ, and I'm honored that I know Zach now, and I really appreciate him writing about my book.

Jerry Martin A former major league ball player who spent a lot of time with the Philadelphia Phillies and, over the years, has become a great friend. Jerry rides on the bus from time to time, and we'll sit up late at night hearing fabulous baseball stories. Jerry checks in on me quite often.

Andy Andrews Andy started his career as a stand-up comic, and he opened quite a few shows for the Oak Ridge Boys in the '70s. Andy has since become one of the premier authors and sought-after public speakers in America. Everybody loves Andy Andrews. He is "The Noticer"!

John Rich Singer, songwriter, producer, musician, patriot, and one of our dearest friends. Along with Big Kenny, their group Big & Rich is one of the top road shows in all of the music business, and it's so cool that John uses his talents for God and country. He is an inspiration on every level.

Gov. Mike Huckabee Quite a few years back, while governor of the great state of Arkansas, Mike called upon the Oak Ridge Boys to take part in the statewide children's educational program. We are still dear friends to this day. Governor Huckabee has become quite a television personality over these years, and he records his popular weekly television show right here in our hometown of Hendersonville, Tennessee.

Dan Rogers Known as "Opry Dan," he literally runs the Grand Ole Opry and is responsible for taking the Opry to new levels every single week. Since my retirement I have not been able to get down to the Opry, so Dan stops by the house once in a while to bring me a gift and greetings from all of my Opry family. I love him!

Peter Rosenberger Life goes on and then sometimes something just slips and everything changes. Because of a devastating accident, Peter's wife's life was changed, and Peter has assumed the caregiver role for four decades. He has since become an advocate for the caregiver, and Mary and I have learned much from him. He is a successful syndicated writer and radio show/podcast host, and his book *A Minute for Caregivers* can be found right here at Fidelis. I appreciate his friendship!

Ace Collins Author of over sixty books, Ace Collins is the ultimate author, and his friendship and inspiration have meant the world to me. Someday perhaps Ace and I will write a book together and change the universe . . . perhaps.

Ben Isaacs The Isaacs—Ben, along with Sonya, Becky, and Lily—may be the best singing group in all of gospel and bluegrass music. Ben himself has produced a lot of music for the Oak Ridge Boys. Over the years we have become closer than brothers. There is nobody like these incredible Christian friends and nobody like brother Ben. Thanks for the prayers!